ood Daniel Barber Thoma

er Aaron Brakke Giorgio B

arreta Constanze Elges K

Gray Rob Henderson Phili

ackson Peter Jahnke Mic

rd Kornberger Kajsa Kraus

wka Adam Marcus Stace

lip Mohr Illich Mujica Ivo

Pierik Alex Pincus Sebast

an Saint Jean Masako Sai

Jasmin Shorter ley S

aele Jose Mun ers

ong Leo Yung Natalie Za

s Barry Jordan Bartlett
Brunetti Dwayne Dancy
Kenny Endo Amy Farina
ip Holley Casey Hughes
hael Johnston Andreas
se Deborah Kully Dong
ey Mariash Jesus Colao
o Nelissen Eun Suk Oh
tian Queney Gregory M.
ito Seiichi Saito Bittor
mit Ana Sotrel Mikkel
Maarten Wessel Nicole
nnettou Ana Zatezalo

AT-INdex

AT-INdex
Winka Dubbeldam

Introduction by
Reed Kroloff

Contributions by
Javier Barreiro Cavestany,
Detlef Mertins, and Michael Speaks

Concept and Design by
COMA Amsterdam/New York

Princeton Architectural Press, New York

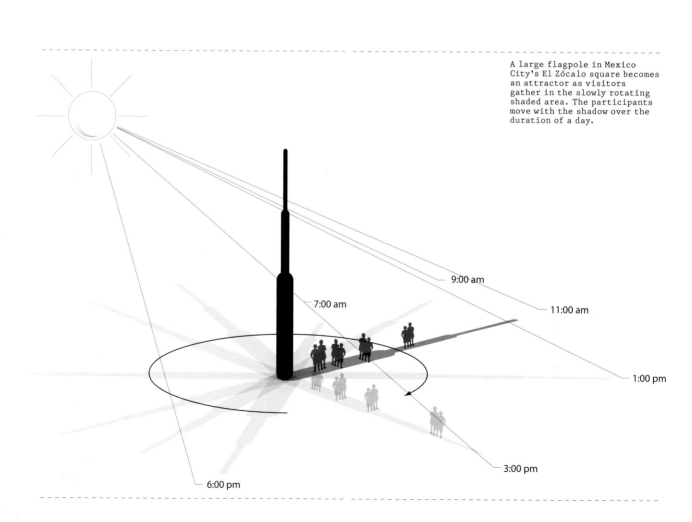

A large flagpole in Mexico City's El Zócalo square becomes an attractor as visitors gather in the slowly rotating shaded area. The participants move with the shadow over the duration of a day.

Meaning-Form:
Architecture as Process

Winka Dubbeldam

The first real challenge lies in the statement and creation of problems (the right problems), the second challenge lies in the discovery of genuine differences in kind; the third, [in] the apprehension of real time. —Gilles Deleuze[1]

BE CURIOUS This notion of the "right" problem as discussed by Gilles Deleuze prioritizes concept development over problem solving, curiosity over absolute knowledge, and immediacy over stasis. This investigative approach has been the red line through the research and design conducted over the last decade at Archi-Tectonics. The work can be described as an open network, a network of projects linked through three fields of investigation: armature, surface, and interface. These fields are not isolated but rather create a synthesis of interests that overlap and inform each other and afford a rethinking, reinvestigating, and regenerating of architectural concepts. The focus is not on form but on the performative, not on aesthetics but on intelligence.

MEANING-FORM The understanding of architecture as "meaning-form" departs from the tradition of architecture as style or form into architecture as process. Large technological developments have often instigated extreme cultural shifts; from the invention of the car in the early twentieth century to mass-media (television) in the 1960s and mass-communication (Internet) in the 1990s, they all changed our view and understanding of the world and dramatically impacted and initiated a global culture. The radical groups in the 1960s, such as Archigram and Superstudio, already envisioned architecture as a dynamic entity, but one that literally moved; Archigram's *Walking City* by Ron Herron is one of the many examples.

At that time, movement was still an expression of the traditional, pervasive mechanistic way of thinking, as opposed to the generative, process-oriented, organismic approach we are now interested in. The basis of the organismic paradigm is the notion that an organism is characterized by its immanent patterns of organization. These organizing phenomena occur on all levels: in social interaction, behavioral processes, and nature.

VIC: VERIFY IN COMPUTER Since its conception in 1994, Archi-Tectonics has operated as a laboratory based on research and design—a philosophy that combines theoretical with pragmatic, research with construction. The computer used as a generative tool rather than a representational or technical device is essential to our practice. The interest lies not in purely abstract formal expressions, but in surface registrations of force fields, smart systems, and programmatic mappings.

In the 1830s, mathematicians already understood that absolute values are relative to behavioral states, and a system-based theory studying complexity and higher-dimensional topology was developed. A topology is a non sequitur, a simplification of the truth of "that which is unthinkable" into four-dimensional life forms. Mathematical philosophy describes this process as "meaning-form," further defined by Edmund Husserl as "phoronomic shapes"[2]; he explains: "phoronomic shapes are formations developed out of tracings of gradual perfection, from which new constructions grow (*phoron*: a combining form meaning bearer, producer)." Phoronomic shapes are thus generative in character; our interest is in this self-generation of meaning-form.

NEVER TRIANGULATE The creation of performative modulations and surfaces is facilitated by the use of generative software. The software generates behavioral patterns, reflected in the sequential differentiation of spatial modules as intelligent registrations. The registrations are distilled in a set of smooth surface deflections, which express the optimal organic modulation for the performance analyzed. This modulation—the generation of spatio-temporal constructs—is system based, and it has led to three distinct areas of research:
—Armature [3rd dimension]: attractors, intelligent structures, generative in character: phoronomic shapes.
—Surface [2.5th dimension]: performative surface inflections with material, bodily characteristics: thing-shapes.
—Interface [4th dimension]: interactive environments are expressed and investigated in gaming interfaces, urban data fields, and real-time interactive installations. This overlap of frame and interface, of the virtual and the real, is where new propositions lie.

ARMATURE The notion of an armature was developed as a series of investigations in performative structures that integrate amenities and generate specific environments. The armature defeats traditional ideas of hierarchical space and rethinks and reconfigures it in performative, intelligent models of occupation. The armature's design-research originates in the Wooster Loft as a free-standing bathroom capsule—a smooth surface deflection with integral bathing amenities that simultaneously acts as a pivot point between public and private zones. This concept evolved in the GT Residence, where the performative aspects of temporal modulations generate a hyperactive core—a centrally located "smart structure" that integrates cooking, bathing, and heating, cooling, and sound systems. The aggregation of the armature's programmatic elements produces a segmented, organic shape, combining smart infrastructure with continuous living environments.

SURFACE The recording of behavioral processes in surface inflections transforms the wall or facade from a separative device into a connective membrane—a smart skin. The relation of skin to body investigates the close connection between artificial intelligence and smart structures. Husserl names these "thing-shapes." Specific to these thing-shapes are their surface registrations that strive for gradual perfection; an essential form becomes recognizable through a method of variation. This emerging variation activates the surface into a hybrid system of recordings. For the Aida Salon, the predecessor to the armature studies, a "smart skin" was developed, in which programmatic inflections create an intelligent wrapper with an organic spatial modulation; function versus program, integral versus integrated, and inclusive versus exclusive are repositioned. The surface blends mathematical behavior with industrial precision into a set of smart layers and integral structures.

INTERFACE The difference between frame and interface lies in the distinction between passive perception and active participation; where the frame defines, the interface mediates. Objective perception operates through interactivity, which exists only through the interface, not the frame. The interface's analogue is found in an informational system, its elements in data. Direct interaction and feedback generate a sequence of animated interactive environments. Flex-City, a gaming interface, was designed after 9-11 as a research environment to rethink the future of Lower Manhattan. It provides an interactive electronic interface that allows the visitor to chose specific parameters that generate different development scenarios for downtown. By combining constant instability (stock market and migration patterns) with permanent adjustment (local politics and tourist behavior), one is able create a cityscape sensitive to Social Flex and Econ Flex.

AND THEN Our research, as it has evolved over the last ten years, is focused on rethinking and reevaluating the question asked and is transformed in the generation of performative models. Our interest is in performance in the traditional sense, such as maintenance-free skins, low energy use, and green structures, but even more in the creation of challenging environments, where the boundary is blurred between industrial-design intelligence and architecture. The attempt is to minimize the influence of bias or prejudice in the experimenter when testing a hypothesis or a theory in order to get to some level of invention. Deleuze describes a similar process as the state of Problem-Ideas, or *Perplication*, where the "idea" is the first principle of the theory of problems. This state of Problem-Ideas, "with their multiplicities and coexistent varieties, their determination of elements, their distribution of mobile singularities, and their formation of ideal series around these singularities," is not unlike the notion of meaning-form as discussed by Husserl.[3] These notions have informed and inspired our design-research, and helped develop innovative spatial constructs and organic modulations, where intelligence is essential, performance integrated, and spontaneous interaction hoped for.

[1] Gilles Deleuze, *Bergsonism* (New York: Zone Books, 1988), 14.
[2] *Edmund Husserl's The Origin of Geometry*, introduction by Jacques Derrida (Lincoln, NE: University of Nebraska, 1962).
[3] Gilles Deleuze, *Difference and Repetition* (New York: Columbia University Press, 1995), 163.

SCALE-FREE NETWORKS There are two conditions that make a network scale-free: growth and preferential attachment. Growth occurs when new nodes appear at any random moment. Preferential attachments are well-connected nodes that attract additional connections. Any network meeting these two conditions will evolve into a scale-free state.

We consider each project an opportunity to create a team of experts with whom we research a specific topic and innovative materials and develop new ideas that, after completion, can dissolve and reorganize into a new project. Links are larger research topics that bind projects into a network of concepts to be developed.

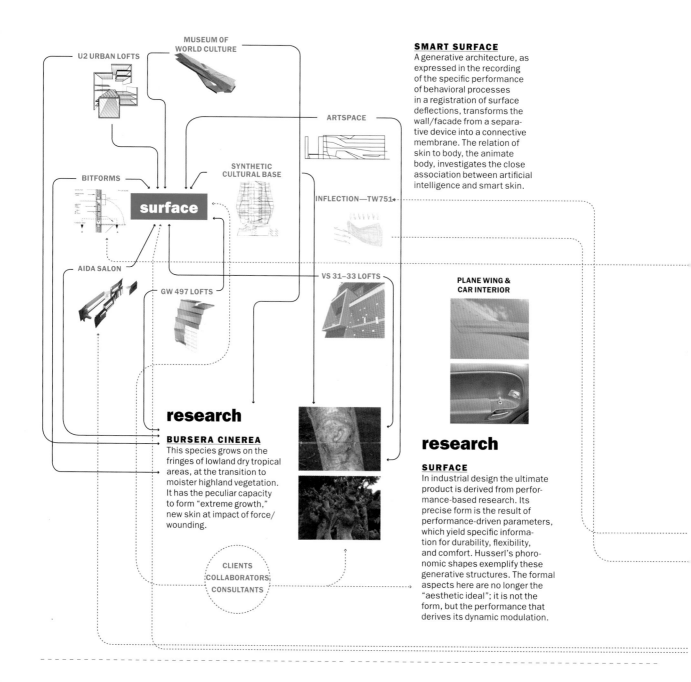

SMART SURFACE
A generative architecture, as expressed in the recording of the specific performance of behavioral processes in a registration of surface deflections, transforms the wall/facade from a separative device into a connective membrane. The relation of skin to body, the animate body, investigates the close association between artificial intelligence and smart skin.

U2 URBAN LOFTS

MUSEUM OF WORLD CULTURE

ARTSPACE

BITFORMS

SYNTHETIC CULTURAL BASE

surface

INFLECTION—TW751

AIDA SALON

GW 497 LOFTS

VS 31–33 LOFTS

PLANE WING & CAR INTERIOR

research

BURSERA CINEREA
This species grows on the fringes of lowland dry tropical areas, at the transition to moister highland vegetation. It has the peculiar capacity to form "extreme growth," new skin at impact of force/wounding.

research

SURFACE
In industrial design the ultimate product is derived from performance-based research. Its precise form is the result of performance-driven parameters, which yield specific information for durability, flexibility, and comfort. Husserl's phoronomic shapes exemplify these generative structures. The formal aspects here are no longer the "aesthetic ideal"; it is not the form, but the performance that derives its dynamic modulation.

CLIENTS COLLABORATORS CONSULTANTS

Hubs are groups of experts, engineers, and consultants that we work with on numerous occasions, dependent on the specific needs of a project. A scale-free-network condition allows for flexibility and efficiency.

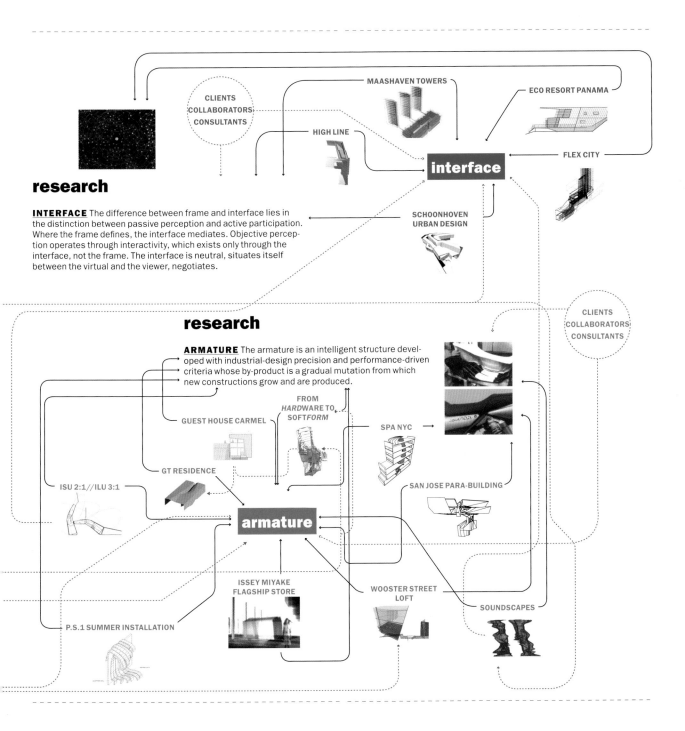

research

INTERFACE The difference between frame and interface lies in the distinction between passive perception and active participation. Where the frame defines, the interface mediates. Objective perception operates through interactivity, which exists only through the interface, not the frame. The interface is neutral, situates itself between the virtual and the viewer, negotiates.

research

ARMATURE The armature is an intelligent structure developed with industrial-design precision and performance-driven criteria whose by-product is a gradual mutation from which new constructions grow and are produced.

CLIENTS COLLABORATORS CONSULTANTS

MAASHAVEN TOWERS

ECO RESORT PANAMA

HIGH LINE

interface

FLEX CITY

SCHOONHOVEN URBAN DESIGN

CLIENTS COLLABORATORS CONSULTANTS

FROM *HARDWARE* TO *SOFTFORM*

GUEST HOUSE CARMEL

SPA NYC

GT RESIDENCE

SAN JOSE PARA-BUILDING

ISU 2:1 // ILU 3:1

armature

ISSEY MIYAKE FLAGSHIP STORE

WOOSTER STREET LOFT

SOUNDSCAPES

P.S.1 SUMMER INSTALLATION

Architecture by the Numbers:
Winka Dubbeldam and the Mathematics of Performance Design

Reed Kroloff

I love generalizations, so here goes: contemporary Dutch architects are data-mad.

At times it seems they get as much—if not more—pleasure analyzing a project as they do designing or building it. This is not to say that the Dutch aren't also inspired designers. Quite the contrary: It's reasonable to argue that they're the best in the world today, as well as the most influential. But look at the books and studies and pamphlets and tracts and articles that accompany nearly every building completed (or even proposed) by a significant contemporary Dutch architect. Page after page of statistics, diagrams, and analysis; beautifully composed, and dizzyingly, almost giddily thorough. There is more architecture in the design of these presentations than there is in most new buildings in the United States.

Thus, the data-driven investigations of New York–based architect Winka Dubbeldam and her firm Archi-Tectonics should come as no surprise to regular observers of the architectural avant-garde, particularly in a time when computational manipulations of the process, form, and material structure of architecture are reshaping the entire field. Dubbeldam is a transplant from Holland who came to the U.S. in 1990 to study at Columbia University, which was then incubating architecture's digital revolution. Working with Stan Allen, Hani Rashid and others, Dubbeldam and a remarkable group of young designers—including Eric Lifton, Greg Pasquarelli, Charles Renfro, Lynn Rice, Lindy Roy, Galia Solomonoff, Dan Wood and others—began to describe the parameters of what would become the profession's next great debate: How will the digital revolution shape architectural discourse, and architecture itself?

For Dubbeldam, that debate was especially seductive in that it not only appealed—naturally—to her Dutch penchant for analysis, but at Columbia at least, also took on some of the character of the complex arguments about theory that had occupied the profession's chattering classes during the last twenty years of the twentieth century, particularly those who came into or near the orbit of *enfant terrible*-for-life, Peter Eisenman. Dubbeldam, in one of the early manifestations of her remarkable knack for being in the right place and arguing the right things to the right people at the right time, had worked for Eisenman between 1992 and 1994, not long after her arrival in New York. Thus her writings and lectures occasionally exhibit the linguistic thickening agents characteristic of that school.

But with Dubbeldam, the density is less contrived. While many architects—including Dubbeldam—label their work as investigations, she means it: she not only resolves the program each time, but also layers it with additional complexity. Look at her project for the National Building Museum's 2004 exhibition, Masonry Variations. For that show, each of four architects was given a typical masonry building product (bricks, lightweight concrete blocks [AAC], stone, and terrazzo) and asked to use it in an atypical way. Dubbeldam's three colleagues each created dazzling formal and structural installations. So did Dubbeldam, and arguably, the fluid concrete gorge she created was the most dramatic and engaging of the bunch, a machined version of the much-photographed Buckskin Gulch at Utah's Paria canyon. She could have stopped there and the exhibition would have been another feather in her cap. But in completing the research on shaping the concrete, Dubbeldam reasoned that in addition to its sculptural potential, the porous lightweight material might have other sensual qualities. Advanced digital analysis of her design, the chamber in which it would be built, and the concrete itself suggested an opportunity to add a fourth dimension to her installation. Working with a sound engineer, Dubbeldam suspended speakers next to the undulating curves of concrete, which scanned the surfaces. The "scrambled" sound waves reorganized as they hit any surface and thus emitted unusual pulses that bounced off and around the shapes, converting the entire assembly into an extraordinary, almost phantasmagorical sound garden.

Needless to say, Masonry Variations generated mountains of data, some of which worked its way into the exhibit, and more of which appears in this book. This kind of analysis, this "richening of the text" if you will, extends to each of Dubbeldam's projects, no matter the scale. For example, the GT Residence has a hallway linking most of its spaces. Like many architects, Dubbeldam refers to the space as a spine. But for her, the description is more than metaphoric. She thickens both the functional and formal complexity of the space so that it quite literally becomes the spinal core of the building—packed with electronics, ductwork, and plumbing: the architectural equivalent of nerves, fluids, and bones. In her Aida Salon, it is the walls that do multiple duty as spatial wrap, power source, and storage device. This investigation of surface as sensory net continues and expands in Dubbeldam's largest and most complex work to date, the GW 497 Lofts in lower Manhattan. Here, there are many readings, beginning with the building itself, which attaches and folds parasitically around an existing restored warehouse. It is not an addition so much as a new organism attaching itself to another. The interface is most visible in the new building's skin, a cascading sheet of bluish glass that folds, bends, and spindles itself to accommodate the new program inside. It is dense with sensors, channels, and filters. And like dermis, it has multiple layers. Though this skin is probably not self-repairing, Dubbeldam undoubtedly is working on that for her next project.

Multivalency, Le Corbusier's familiar term for double-functioning, is thus multiplied, and multiplied again in the "performative" world of digital architecture: one assesses an architectural object or component not just for its beauty or its utility, but for its capacity to allow—and even encourage—change. Dubbeldam's performative unit, or walls, or skin perform multiple actual and representational functions, and may perform a different set in the future. It is in creating this flexibility that beauty is born, rather than as a goal unto itself. In other words, aesthetics is no longer a point of departure in the design process; it is a byproduct of analysis.

For Dubbeldam, this is of course an ideal condition. Her buildings and installations are sensual, handsome things. At the same time, they can be evaluated objectively against equation sets derived without regard for esthetic implication. It's a numbers game, in a sense, but one with beautiful implications.

AR·MA·TURE n. [L. *armatura*, arms, equipment; all senses from that of "armored, protected"] **1.** any protective covering: see ARMOR (senses 1 & 2) **2.** any part or structure of an organism useful for defense or offense, as claws, teeth, burs, etc. **3.** a soft iron bar placed across the poles of a magnet to keep it from losing magnetic power **4.** a) the laminated iron core with wire wound around it in which electromotive force is produced by magnetic induction in a generator or motor: usually a revolving part, but in an alternating-current machine often stationary b) the vibrating part in an electric relay or bell **5.** Sculpture a framework for supporting the plastic material in modeling

—*Webster's New World Dictionary of the American Language*, 2nd ed., *s.v.* "Armature."

arma ture

MEANING-FORM, a term used by Edmund Husserl, best describes the performative origin and generative effect of the armature.[1] The research in the generation of the armature moves away from pure formal aesthetics; it is not the form, but the performance that derives the armature's modulation. For example, here, at a busy intersection in Mexico City, a person has found a peaceful sleeping spot that allows a moment of privacy within the urban turmoil. The planter spontaneously becomes an urban attractor, generating new use and an alternate environment.

Appropriating the intelligence of industrial design, which is always reactive to and an integral part of new organizational systems and behaviors, the armature encapsulates program and generates overlapping environments. It integrates strategies of performative analysis, three-dimensional modeling and rapid prototyping, and negotiates inhabitant with built environment through its organic modulation. This modulation—the generation of organic spatial constructs—is no longer a static device, or object, but a set of mobile sections, sequential variations, and transmutations: surface registrations of force fields, smart systems, and programmatic mappings.

[1] *Edmund Husserl's The Origin of Geometry*, introduction by Jacques Derrida (Lincoln, NE: University of Nebraska, 1962).

Lyrical Architectonics

Detlef Mertins

It seems to me that the lyrical work is originally linked to the animated dance, the architectonic work to the body of the star earth, which it wants to beautify through rebuilding. —Adolf Behne[1]

These words, written in 1919 by the Berlin critic Adolf Behne take us back to a time when being could still be divided into two mutually exclusive categories—animate and inanimate, lyrical and architectonic, structure and event. Prior to the Great War, an exemplar of Behne's distinction could be found in Emile Jaques-Dalcroze's Institute of Rhythmic Gymnastics in the garden city of Hellerau, built in 1911 by Heinrich Tessenow. Here, Tessenow's resolutely immobile, prismatic, and architectonic classicism provided a foil for the fluid and expressive movements of the students, at times ecstatic and at times agonistic. It offered a serene framework for rendering thoughts and emotions plastically in time as in space. The exercises developed by Dalcroze sought to attune students to musical rhythms through physical movement but quickly extended to the entire personality of the individual and, more broadly still, to the restoration of life rhythms under the adverse conditions of modernization. Coordinating muscle and nerve responses also promoted coordination among moving bodies and participation in the dynamics of nature.

Behne's observation implicitly reiterated Nietzsche's influential distinction in *The Birth of Tragedy* between the Dionysian and Apollinian arts—music and sculpture.[2] Nietzsche considered these to be manifestations of a duality found first in nature, then in culture, between the impulse to self-abnegation through intoxication and the impulse to self-affirmation through the pursuit of beauty in the inner world of dream. Rather than codifying this distinction—which itself reiterated the opposition of chaos and order, creation and duration—Nietzsche's goal was to understand the birth of Greek tragedy in which these impulses intermingle. More than this, Nietzsche used the example of Greek tragedy to delineate a model of an artist who worked in both dream and ecstasies: "So we may perhaps picture [the artist] sinking down in his Dionysian intoxication...and we may imagine how, through Apollinian dream-inspiration, his own state, i.e., his oneness with the inmost ground of the world, is revealed to him in a *symbolical dream image.*" In contrast, Behne promoted a clear division, favoring what he saw as the new emphasis on architectonics in cubist art over the lyricism of expressionism. It would remain for other critics to recognize that by incorporating motion, time, and the dynamics of viewing into the representation of objects, cubism—but also futurism, suprematism, and constructivism—marked a shift in the very conception of what an object is, a shift in which body and motion, figure and ground, time and space were no longer mutually exclusive but imbricated in one another, a collapse integral to the dynamic unfolding of immanence. In retrospect, the figure of the artist or architect as a Dionysian Apollo points to the recurrence over the last century of the dream of a lyrical architectonic. From dancing crystals to voids of potentiality, from immersive abstract environments to immersion in self-organizing systems, all these are images that play out the unfulfilled desire for an architectonics of music, dance, and animation, of rhythmic incorporation and virtuality.

Winka Dubbeldam's From *Hard*Ware to Soft*Form* is the latest stage in the transformation of an idea from one project to another in her recent work. Its starting point may be seen in the Aida Salon in New York, an ethereal, crystalline interior, irregular and dynamic in shape, something between a cave, a space station, and a cloud. The faceted and folded surfaces of the architectonic shell are mounted to a structure of bent ribs that also houses an infrastructure of plumbing, wiring, heating, and air-conditioning. Despite the strength of its image, the form recedes to open a void of potentiality. Quietly it supports the activities and dreams of its occupants—the cutting, shaping, and treatment of hair that magically rejuvenates the spirit.

The next project, GT Residence, in Kent, New York, began by reversing the relationship between space and support, giving shape first to a core armature that contains the main structure and services of the house. This armature extracts the enveloping surface and infrastructure of the salon, reducing it in size and transforming it to become an object. But it is a special kind of object, one that extends life-support and space-defining vectors into the environment around it. The outer form of the house emerged as an organic extension of the armature into the natural site, creating spaces around it that enable the life of the occupants to unfold in a coordinated interplay with their milieu. To complicate things further, the armature also contains the kitchen and bathroom within it, like capsules, but with views to the forest and sky beyond.

The installation, From *Hard*Ware to Soft*Form*, originally designed for the Frederieke Taylor Gallery, transforms the idea of armature once again by isolating the core of the GT Residence and presenting it as an object detached from any specific conditions, floating freely in the space of the gallery. As an object, this armature is at once infrastructural, space containing, and space generating. But in the gallery it exists only as a projected three-dimensional image—lighter than life and set in motion. As image, it is imbued with an additional intelligence that allows it to respond to the stimuli of visitors while shifting and mutating according to its own inner rhythms and choreography. Rendering its volume in slices interlaced with plumbing suggests the structural ribs of a battleship or a starship. At once anachronistic and futuristic, it evokes both the mechanical past and the neurological future of an infrastructural conception of architecture. Plastic and interactive, responsive and synergistic, this architecture will not only serve us but also dance with us and envelop us. Dubbeldam's Armature stages an encounter with an animate and lyrical architectonic as seductive and yet fearsome as swimming with a whale.

[1] Adolf Behne, *Wiederkehr der Kunst* [The Return of Art] (Leipzig: Kurt Wolff, 1919), 20; translation by author.
[2] Friedrich Nietzsche, *The Birth of Tragedy*, trans. Walter Kaufmann (New York: Random House, 1967), 38.

Type   Residence
Location   Carmel, New York
Area   3,000 sq. ft.
Year   2002

GT Residence

At the Croton Reservoir in upstate New York, the hills tumble into the lake. Simultaneously soft and hard, rolling and jagged, the lakefront alternates green patches with craggy, rock formations. The GT Residence is built into this landscape. Connecting to the lake and surroundings through cantilevering terraces, the house is modern, functional, and moderate in nature.

No longer concerned with a formal language, but with added intelligence and **PERFORMANCE-DRIVEN** precision, the house is designed from the inside out. Developed through a study on the performative aspects of hyperactive versus leisure domestic activity, its structural center resides in a generative core, the **ARMATURE**. A centrally located "smart structure," it integrates the kitchen, bathrooms, storage space, heating and cooling ducts, environmental controls, and a central music system. The aggregation of the armature's elements produces a segmented, organic shape, resulting in the self-generation of "meaning-form."

The armature functions not only as an infrastructural and circulatory unit but also as a generative element, directing interior movement and molding the surfaces it connects to. Its irregular shape distorts the straight geometry of the exterior shell; the roof warps to conform to the core's segmentation and the "house-as-pure-box" softens, tilts, and fragments. The armature, hyperactive in its function, deactivates the surrounding spaces, now designated as "**LOUNGING VOIDS**." It defies the traditional hierarchical relationship between hallways and rooms, and creates a continuity of overlapping environments and integral adjacencies. Architecture becomes a responsive medium—responsive to the organic shapes, human forms, and functions it houses.

The ground floor, constructed of rough stone collected on site, is partially recessed into the hillside. It has direct access to the lake via a low, secluded path with a retaining wall, leading to an outdoor shower and "hot tub" built into the rocks. The second floor cantilevers out over the stone base toward the lake. This volume of zinc, wood, and glass sits at an angle, **TWISTED** to procure an uninterrupted view of the water and to capture maximum sunlight. The sun enters through glass planes that are integrated into a continuous wall-to-roof surface, channeling light into various areas of the house. Where the roof bends to meet the armature, glass planes replace the zinc roof to form of a continuous skylight. At the end of the armature, the glass panels fold into the wall, creating a transparent shower room suspended in the trees. The architecture is responsive to both environmental regulators and natural environments.

The GT Residence exemplifies the concepts of interdependent layers (wall/glass/roof/glass/armature), efficiency of use (infrastructural core), and negotiation of means (interior/exterior). By forming the house around the armature, a supply response to precise living requirements, a new, intelligent domestic environment is created.

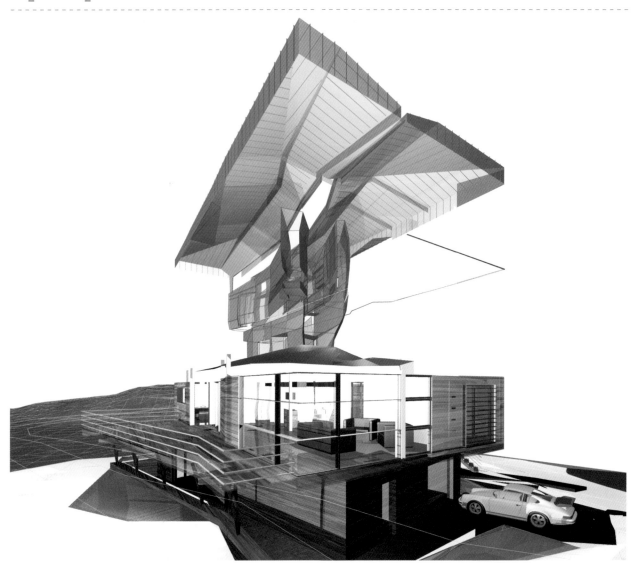

TWIST The main floor sits at an angle on a recessed stone base and cantilevers over the rocks and the lake. Continuous surfaces of cedar, zinc, and glass are chosen for their insulation value and low maintenance requirements. As they slowly weather to similar tints, they dissolve into the surrounding landscape; this camouflage strategy allows for fluid integration.

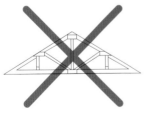

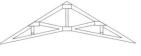

The scissor truss, usually used in large-span design, is appropriated, allowing the spatial undulation to be visible inside and outside. The lightweight truss has an average spacing of 2 feet but varies up to 4 feet on center.

The average combined dead and live loads are 45 pounds per square foot. Spans, typically 20 to 32 feet, can be up to 50 feet in some applications. It provides flexibility in the design and strength in the structure of the roof.

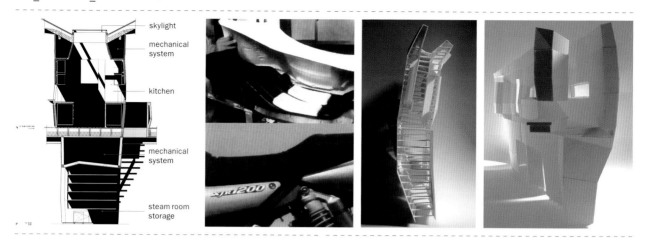

skylight

mechanical system

kitchen

mechanical system

steam room storage

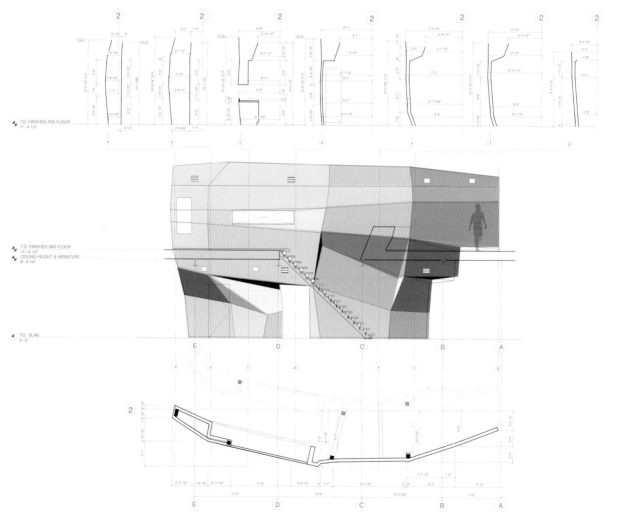

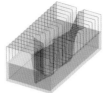
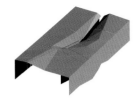
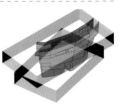

The motorbike seat mold (left) is the imprint of the machine to the body; it negotiates comfort with speed, steel with flesh. Its built-in intelligence allows for the perfect fit during high-endurance trips.

ARMATURE The armature is a centrally located circulatory and generative element that integrates hygienic amenities, heating and cooling systems, a central sound system, and a fireplace into a "smart" environment.

The insertion of a hyperactive core not only adds efficiency to the performance of the house, but also activates the center of the space and becomes an attractor; surfaces warp, bend, and fold toward the armature, creating undulating roof surfaces, which are registered both on the inside and the outside of the house.

PERFORMANCE The morphing of the armature's performative requirements produces a segmented, organic shape. Here, the bathroom entry reveals the folded surfaces that configure the bathing programs and the continuous skylight above, where nature and light reflect in the smooth surfaces—bathing under the stars.

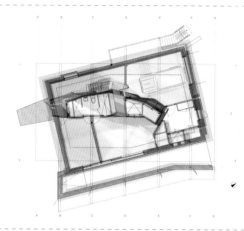

basement

The structure is designed to allow for a continuous glass skylight without any structural beams crossing it. The skylight runs throughout the whole house; wall surfaces envelop bathing amenities and fragment to meet the skylight above.

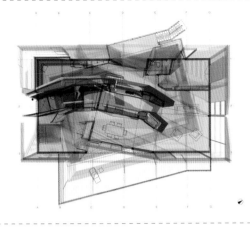

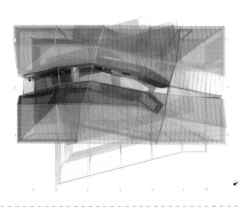

first floor

roof

Undulating zinc and glass
roof surfaces create a spatial
continuity and pull light rays
deep into the space.

LOUNGING VOIDS The insertion of the hyperactive zones in the armature integrates bathing, cooking, and installation spaces with the living and dining areas unfolding around it as lounging voids. As a result, differentiated areas, or fields of occupation, are formed replacing the traditional hallway/room configuration.

Descending the stairs along the armature's modulated walls, one gets a glimpse of the guest house in the trees.

SUSPEND The wood structure of the guest house is suspended off the stone volume of the two-car garage. Its split-level configuration hovers just above the surrounding topography—not unlike a backpack, it seems to travel light.

Type	Residence/guest house and garage
Location	Carmel, New York
Area	1,500 sq. ft.
Year	2001

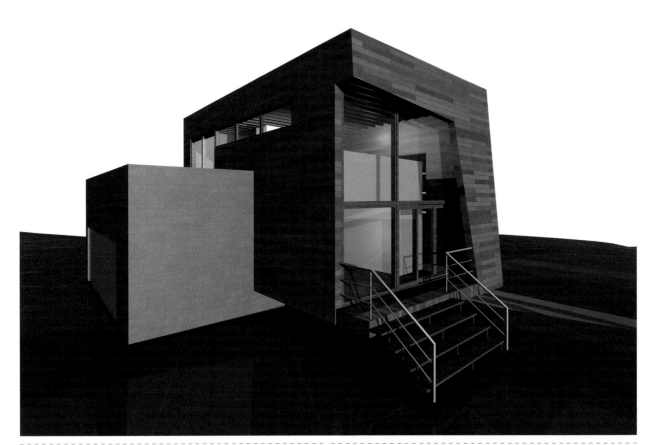

Guest House Carmel

The Guest House was envisioned as a light wood structure **SUSPENDED** as a backpack from the stone volume of the garage. Seen as the alter-ego of the larger, main house, it is similar in materials and a kind, small, basic version of its more sophisticated other. The 1,500-square-foot building accommodates a two-car garage and split-level guest house. The garage, as a base, is constructed of rough stone collected from the site. This simple base intersects and supports the wood-frame guest house volume. The tilted wood-and-glass structure hovers over the ground,

and the living area, located on the second floor, yields an amazing view of the lake. The dining and kitchen area leads out to the large terrace on the garage roof, providing an overview of the site. A full-height interior void connects to the sleeping area, with access to a small porch and the surrounding nature. Sunlight enters through high glass planes integrated into a continuous surface. The double-height entrance area is made up of layers of wood screens, large glass setbacks, and long felt curtains that create a soft boundary between interior and exterior spaces.

ground floor

second floor

The stone volume supports and intersects the suspended wood volume of the split-level guest house. The facade is a set of layers; a wood screen and a double-height glass wall sit in front of a double-height entrance space.

The living functions are inverted; the living room is situated on the second floor with a great view over the lake (below left) and a terrace on top of the garage and the bedroom is downstairs with direct access to the porch and the lake for a morning swim (below right).

Sequential section cuts through the suspended structure of the guest house

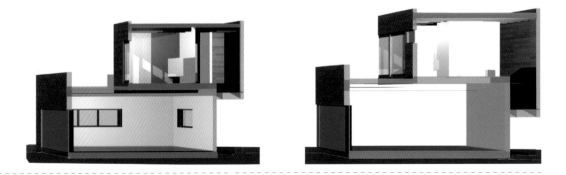

SMART SYSTEMS The foundation system is a new hyper-insulated mold; the integration of insulation and formwork results in a temporary artwork in the landscape.

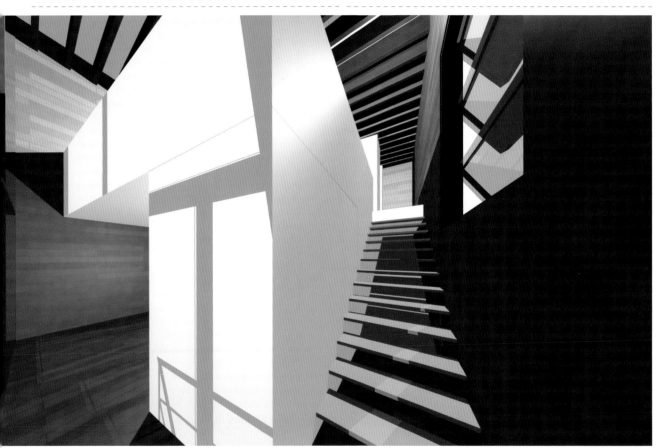

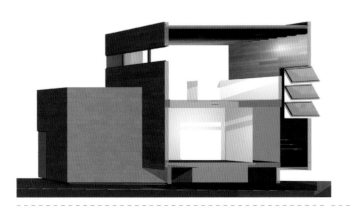

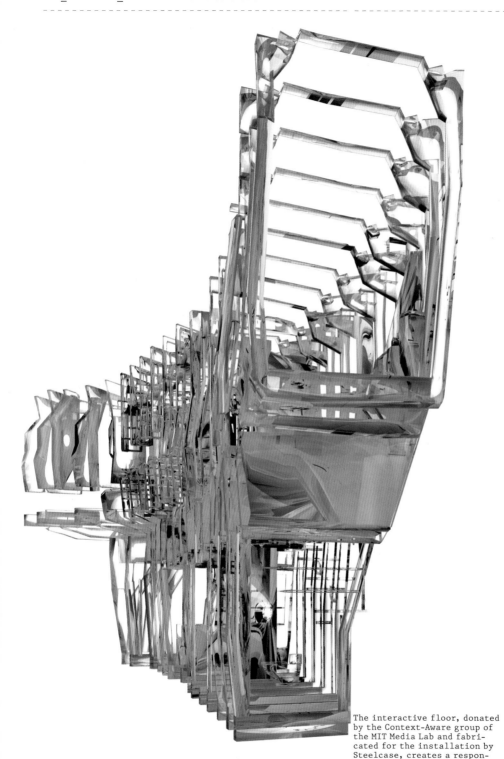

Type   Interactive installation
Location   Frederieke Taylor Gallery,
            New York City; Art & Idea
            Gallery, Mexico City
With   Ted Selker, Winslow
            Burleson, and Ernesto
            Arroyo of the MIT Media
            Lab, Cambridge
Area   1,100 sq. ft.
Year   September 2002;
            August 2004

The interactive floor, donated by the Context-Aware group of the MIT Media Lab and fabricated for the installation by Steelcase, creates a responsive environment that reacts to the movements of the visitor through "triggers" integrated in the steel floor tiles. They cause a series of real-time digital transformations in the projection space to occur. The 96 Pin I/O Board triggers are connected to 2' x 2' pressure-activated floor panels with a Macromedia Director interface.

From *Hard*Ware to Soft*Form*

From *Hard*Ware to Soft*Form* is a three-dimensional digital interactive installation exhibited in the Frederieke Taylor Gallery in New York City in September 2002, and in the Art & Idea Gallery in Mexico City in August 2004. The invitation for an exhibition at the Taylor Gallery presented a great opportunity to research and test a concept rather than create a display of built work. This research focused on the tension between object and **ENVIRONMENT** as it occurs in the "armature," which in its true form originates as a modulated core for the GT Residence. The armature functions as an infrastructural and circulatory unit, but even more as a generative structure. The gallery installation examines this tension and the consequential mutation of the object into the environment it generates.

The resulting holographic projection space proved quite a challenge; seven months, four sponsors, and a lot of investment later, it manifested in the gallery as a real-time interactive, electronic environment. Initiated by the gallery's visitor, sensors, or **TRIGGERS**, distributed in floor panels developed by the Context-Aware Computing Group of the MIT Media Lab, activate the projected object—a dissection of an organic unit that expands, contracts, and envelops—and transform it into an environment of light, speed, and sound. As the visitor moves through the installation, each of the four **SENSOR FIELDS** ("push me," "stroke me," "twist me," and "become me") transmits data to the computer, which in turn alters the projected space and the sound frequencies.

The transformation of the armature as built form in the GT Residence into an animated environment required a mathematical abstraction; a mathematical method, used to analyze higher-dimensional behavior in digital simulations, was employed. As the armature is activated, it is sliced, animated, and programmed with varying levels of elasticity and speed and deformation values. Containing a built-in memory, the three-dimensional model is abstracted and transformed, but always returns to its original shape, the armature; the mutation begins again only when triggered.

Environment mutation is further enhanced by sampled sound frequencies. Created by a composer specifically for this installation, the sound space is generated by four sound fields that carry the same frequency distortion as the animations. Each sound is sampled differently and maintains its own character. In addition, localized hypersonic sound beams, developed by Robotics International, scramble the sound waves as they leave the speaker. As a plane is encountered, the waves reorganize, causing the sound to project from that surface and creating a three-dimensional sound space.

The real-time interaction of the installation not only challenges the relationship between viewer and object, but also reinvestigates the armature's "objectness." An ambiguous animated environment of light and sound ensues, enveloping the visitor in the gallery's confines.

In *The Origin of Geometry*, philosopher Edmund Husserl states, "Proceeding from the factual, an essential form becomes recognizable through a method of variation." Indefinite forms strive for gradual perfection through digital registration. The generative aspect of the armature produces a hybrid system of layering; the politics of layering, creasing, and wrapping thus stimulates zones and environments where boundaries are negotiated and distinctions are blurred.

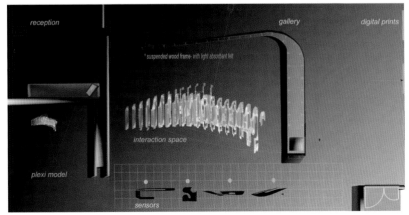

TRIG-GER n. **1.** a small lever or part which when pulled or pressed releases a catch, spring, etc. **2.** in firearms, a small lever pressed back by a finger to activate the firing mechanism **3.** an act, impulse, etc. that initiates an action, series of events, etc. —vt. **1.** to fire or activate by pulling a trigger. **2.** to initiate (an action); set off [the fight that triggered the riot] —quick on the trigger [Colloq.] **1.** quick to fire a gun. **2.** quick to act, understand, retort, etc.; alert

—*Webster's New World Dictionary of the American Language*, 2nd ed., s.v. "Trigger."

BECOME ME   PUSH ME   STROKE ME   TWIST ME

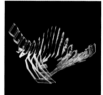

SENSOR FIELDS Four trigger fields, "stroke me," "push me," "become me," and "twist me," when activated, transform the armature according to different levels of elasticity, speed, and sound.

TW452

Nine frames of the animated "twist me" trigger show the different stages of deformation of the armature. The deformation has a built-in memory; it always returns to its original form.

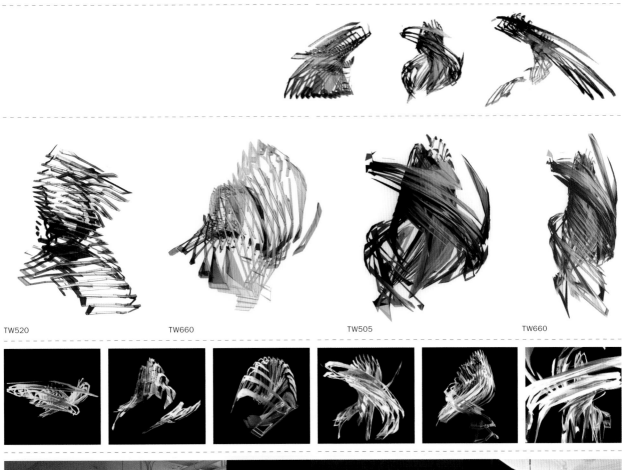

TW520   TW660   TW505   TW660

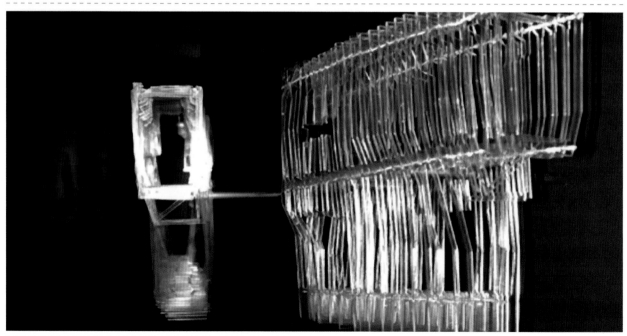

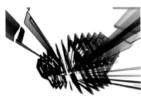

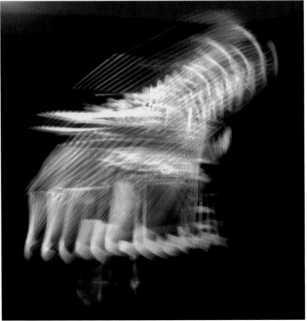

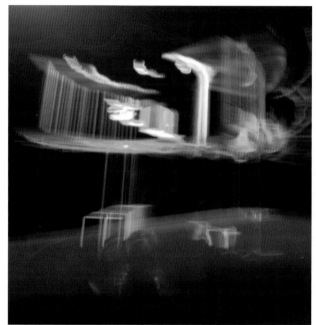

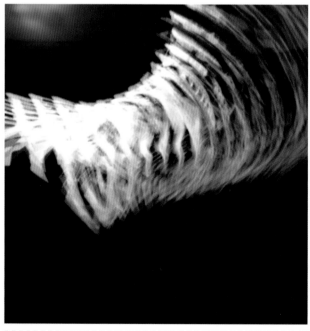

ENVIRONMENT The tension between object (armature) and environment is explored in this interactive installation. As the visitor triggers the animation, they instigate the real-time transformation of the armature. The armature's animation in an environment of light, speed, and sound changes the way the viewer perceives the projected space, critiques the armature's objectness, and envelops the participant in this new digital realm.

Location   New York City
Type   Health spa and gym
Area   15,000 sq. ft.
Year   2004

COCOON A translucent volume is suspended through five floors from the roof to the lobby ceiling. Its dynamic, light, mesh-like structure encloses the main stairway, both penetrating and connecting each level, and terminates as the rooftop cafe.

Spa NYC

The health focus of the new-age baby boomer has led to an explosion of holistic centers, gyms, and spas in metropolitan areas all around the world. Hotels, especially, are the new hot spots for cool nightclubs, gourmet restaurants, and health spas. Our client is planning to develop a spa in a five-story townhouse owned by the Plaza Athenee located on the Upper East Side in New York City. The townhouse is situated directly adjacent to the hotel and although it maintains its own street entrance, it connects to the hotel on the second floor.

The Spa is designed from the top down, with a large translucent ellipse-shaped volume as the primary generative element. This volume penetrates the roof, creating the roof garden and juice bar, and is suspended in the full height of the space as a lucent **COCOON** with stairs and bridges connecting floors and treatment zones. Translucent textured surfaces allow the doubly warped skin of the infrastructural unit to provide a very light and well-lit area. The softly glowing cocoon is seductive and pleasurable, referring to the notion of perfect skin. The floors have generous mezzanines for interior connection, as well as large open areas for relaxation. The ground level is a double-height space containing the lobby, shop, and spa treatments. Yoga, massage, and body and facial treatment rooms are located throughout each floor, always providing ample daylight and fresh air. A bamboo garden in the back and terraces along the garden facade create a filter of green space.

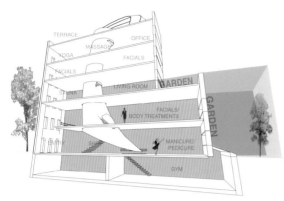

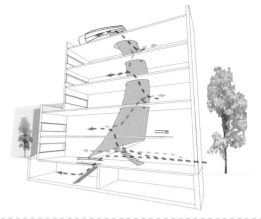

roof terrace

third floor

The lobby/entry area will be transformed into a dramatic double-height space into which the stair cocoon ascends and descends. Mezzanines allow for a spatial and visual experience of the building as a whole.

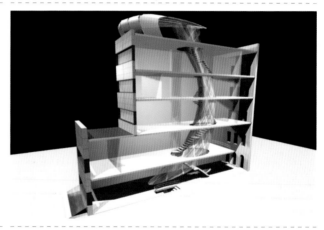

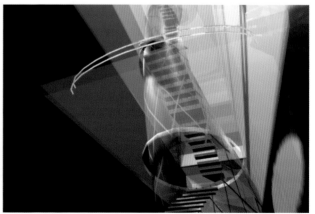

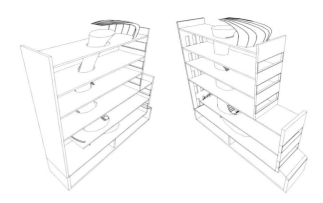

The facade of the landmark townhouse located in the Upper East Side of Manhattan is preserved with the new insertion of an expanded building structure for the spa. The back face is a lightweight aluminum-and-glass panel wall, which creates generous band windows and access to roof terraces. This industrially designed facade will integrate heating, cooling, shades, and metal grilles to filter light and views.

second floor

ground floor

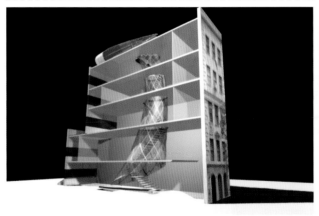

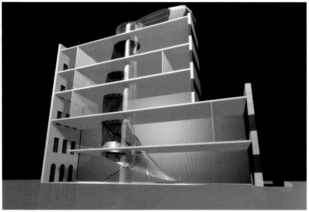

Type	Media Table/lounging units; competition
Location	Walker Art Center, Minneapolis, Minnesota
Year	2002

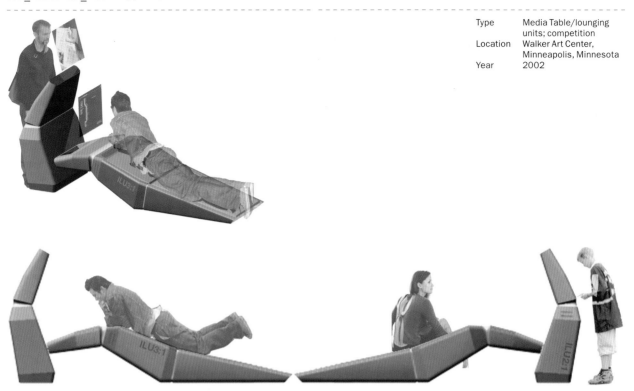

ISU 2:1//ILU 3:1 Two types of telematic units are created, the ISU 2:1, a standing, active unit and the ILU 3:1, an extended lounging unit. Above these modular units holographic information screens are suspended in the lobby, instigating general discussions and an integration within a larger (global) discourse. The different modulations allow for differentiation in the clustering.

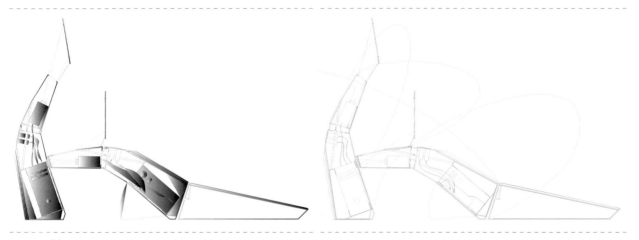

ISU 2:1//ILU 3:1

The Walker Art Center collection has integrated works with dance and other installation performances since the 1950s. This aspect places the Walker ahead of much of the art world and precipitates its latest advancement toward the ephemeral art of the digital, its New Media Initiative. This initiative invites architects and designers to develop an interactive digital system, a Telematic Table, to facilitate museum-based social and informational interchange.

This new concept development for a Telematic Table is an obvious continuation of the Walker's cultural position; the visitor becomes an integral part of the ongoing collection of installation art. The program of the table seemed limited, however, as the visitor's interaction is confined to one location in the museum lobby. The table here is reinterpreted as a landscape: a series of relaxed, comfortable seating units, each with a wireless suspended data screen. The challenge is to organize these units in a casual setting that encourages an exchange of information ruled by interactive retrieval.

As the electronic world becomes progressively miniaturized and digital interfaces thinner and more refined, the duration of use and the needs for physical comfort increase; hence social comfort and information combine in this "infor-mation landscape." The unit design acknowledges this need in a simple, but technological and expandable, manner. To promote spatial dynamics and differentiation, two lounging data units have been developed: the Interactive Lounging Unit **(ILU 3:1)** and the Interactive Standing Unit **(ISU 2:1)**. The ISU 2:1 is composed of sections one and two of the ILU 3:1, allowing for extensive modularity and affordable reproduction of the units. Section three of the lounging unit is unique to this type and can be used as a footrest.

Each of these "soft-body" units can be used independently, situated in clusters, or integrated as part of a series, stimulating visitors to explore and enjoy the media services of the Walker (Gallery9, net.art, and various extensions of the New Media Initiative), while sharing information with others. A series, made up of two or more units, creates a landscape of horizontal seating and vertical data screens—an organic pattern of interactive social space; the table as object is transformed into the table as **FIELD**.

New technologies are integrated in the organic/ergonomic forms: USB ports for syncing; IR (infrared) ports and more advanced 802.11 ports for sending and receiving CHTML-based information; and large touch pads for interaction with the information on the screen. Ultimate seating comfort is

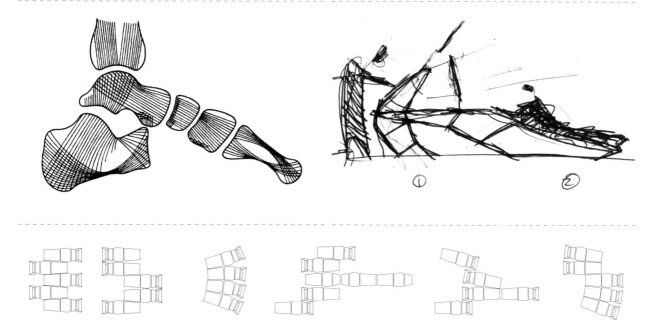

provided while accessing the touch screens, which, through holographic projection, "float" the information above the unit, maintaining a high-resolution interface that is viewable in broad daylight. The layering of this information, and thus interests, in space creates communication among users. The visitor is able to relax, lean, lounge, and retrieve information concurrently—allowing multiple intellectual and physiological postures to rest side by side.

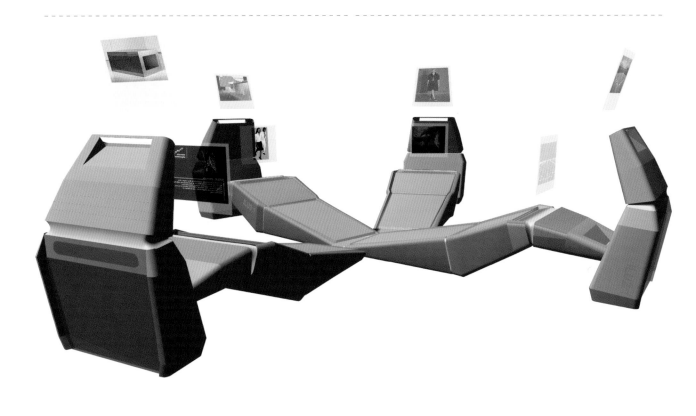

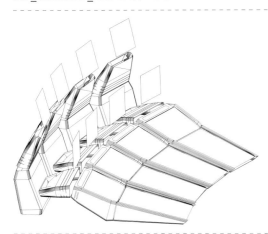

FIELD Rather than a singular media table, we have chosen to design a field condition—an assembly of multiple units that create an organic pattern and an interactive social space. Above the units holographic information screens are loosely suspended—reasons to discuss and integrate within a larger (global) discussion.

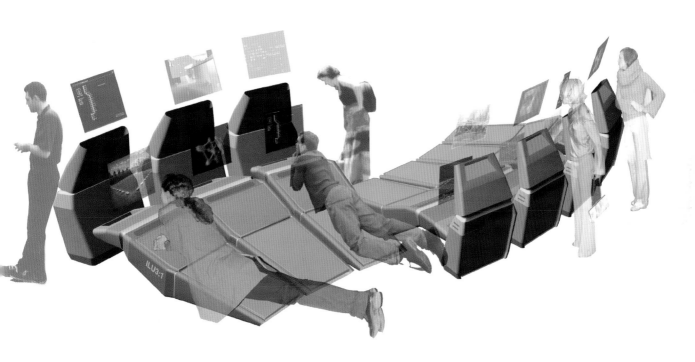

Cluster patterns differentiate the use and density of the lobby area. Information densi- fies and the clusters adapt.

FRINGE A set of lounging seating units are suspended off the existing
courtyard walls, creating an interactive fringe condition (also visible from the
street) and allowing for multiple use and interpretation.

Type	Courtyard installation; invited competition
Location	P.S.1, Long Island City, New York
Area	17,500 sq. ft.
Year	2001

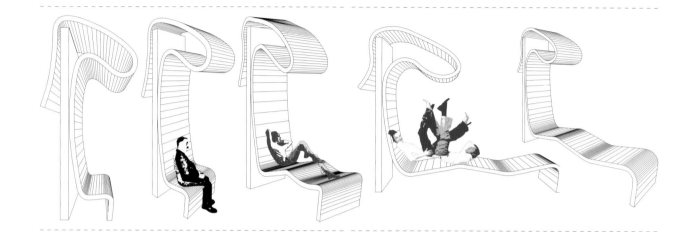

P.S.1 Summer Installation

Evolving social structure in communities of agents through meme evolution, artificial life models can provoke insight about our own world. —Steve Banks

The request of the curators of P.S.1 to create a "tropical deserted island paradise" for the summer 2001 installation was as intriguing as it was unclear. Our initial approach was to analyze the definitions of each of the words. We discovered the following interesting deviations in meaning:

tropic: combining form meaning; turning, changing or otherwise reacting to a specific stimulus; *deserted*: to join, place in a row (Greek: fasten in rows); *island*: "water land," anything like an island in position and isolation. A traffic island. A tissue or cluster of cells differing from surrounding tissue in formation; *paradise*: heaven, abode of the blessed, park, garden. An enclosure, to knead clay, to build a wall. Great beauty, great happiness.[1]

This series of descriptions was randomly sampled in order to script a specific scenario for the installation. The scenario read: *a clustering of self-organizational islands placed in a row, reactive to pressures, with great beauty*.

The P.S.1 summer event can draw up to seven thousand people at any given time. This event density creates spontaneous self-organization; people group and regroup according to local attractors (DJ, music, drinks, fountain, lounging areas), forming "**EVENT FIELDS**." A particle animation was used to simulate and thus analyze these reactive event fields in the P.S.1 courtyard. The creation of a simplified social model allowed us to scrutinize and map out unpredictable

group dynamics. For the simulation of this event, five basic principles were followed:

proximity: simple space-time computations; quality: response to environment; diversity: wide range of activities; stability: no change in mode of operation when environment changes; and adaptability: change in behavior when opportune.

In the animation process, various equations were calculated as the different attractors were input and reacted to. Large cluster concentrations formed throughout the main space of the courtyard and new areas opened up at its edges. The emergence of empty pockets provided an opportune moment to insert subsets of seating units as "**FRINGES**" and "islands," while allowing the event the free space it needed.

The event generates the center space and the installation negotiates the edge. The units, suspended from the courtyard walls, act as an armature and form continuous, relaxed, and supple seating that moves with the visitors. The "flapping" can be seen from the street, a registration of activities inside, connecting the event with the city. The seating units bulge on the top to create shadow folds and stretch out to become extra seating for one, two, three, or more people. Throughout the space the units adapt to and create each event space. For example, at the building entry, the fringe moves up to become a temporal bar; in the seating area, a fountain reacts electronically to the music; and in the courtyard, an extra-large unit is generated for the DJ.

[1] *Webster's New World Dictionary of the American Language*, 2nd ed., s.vv. "Tropic," "Deserted," "Island," "Paradise."

EVENT FIELD The summer installation for P.S.1, an event space with DJs, beach, and pool areas, draws a great amount of visitors (7,000 on a typical Saturday afternoon). Multiple interactions, resulting from activity attractors, will form social swarms/clusters. A particle animation was created to simulate and designate event fields and to find potential empty pockets. These pockets became the space for intervention—the "fringe" condition.

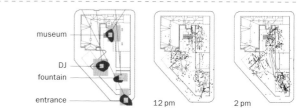

museum

DJ

fountain

entrance

12 pm

2 pm

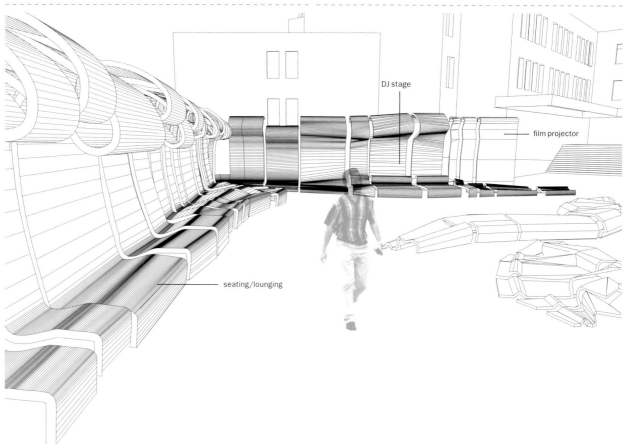

DJ stage

film projector

seating/lounging

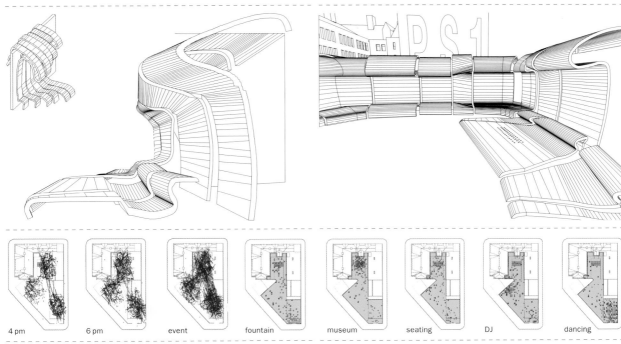

| 4 pm | 6 pm | event | fountain | museum | seating | DJ | dancing |

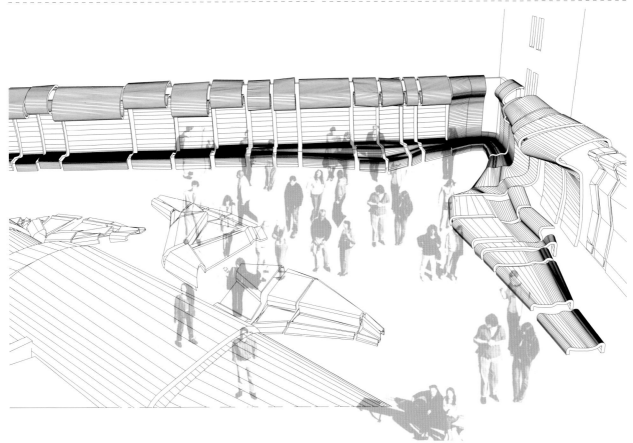

Type	Interactive installation: Masonry Variations
Location	National Building Museum, Washington, D.C.
Area	2,500 sq. ft.; 18 ft. ceiling
Year	October 2003–April 2004

La Poème électronique by composer Edgard Varese was translated into hyperbolic paraboloids (right) by composer/architect Iannis Xenakis for Le Corbusier's 1958 Philips Pavilion.

A specific sound piece was composed for the SoundScapes exhibition space (below).

The sound emitted by the audio speaker, developed by International Robotics, is perceived only by those in direct contact with its path. The speakers scramble the sound waves, which reorganize upon hitting a surface—in this case, the soft solids themselves.

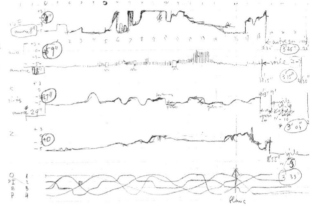

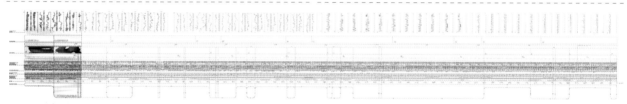

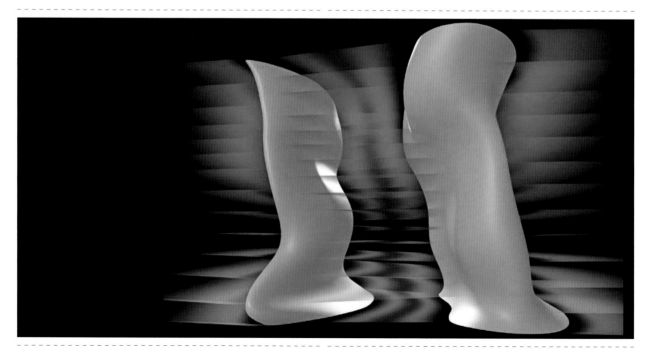

SoundScapes

SoundScapes was designed and constructed for the Masonry Variations exhibition at the National Building Museum in Washington, D.C. Curated by Stanley Tigerman, the concept of the exhibit called for a rethinking and reinterpretation of traditional building materials, in our case Autoclaved Aerated Concrete (AAC)—a soft, malleable concrete block. How can these materials be used in the future, through contemporary or even avant-garde research in architecture? AAC intrigued us because of its light, spongy quality and its ability to easily form and transform—what we considered a "**SOFT SOLID**."

In the past, lightweight architecture has been inexorably connected with sound and acoustics. The Philips Pavilion by Le Corbusier in Brussels is an innovative example of such use. Constructed for the World Expo of 1958, the structure was based on *La Poème électronique* by composer Edgard Varese. The score was translated into hyperbolic paraboloids by revolutionary Greek composer/architect Iannis Xenakis, yielding the expressive form of the pavilion. The 1963 design for the Berlin Philharmonic by architect Hans Scharoun and Vito Acconci's 1990–91 Bra installation in New York City are other impressive examples of a similar concept.

All of these works were created from a lightweight material, such as a membrane, and sound was the primary inspiration behind the design conception. Consequently, these skin-like structures became organic reflections of sound that form and define new spatial experiences and atmospheres. The visitor in this sense not only occupies the space but also becomes an integral part of the acoustic experience, altering the environment and inevitably making these spaces interactive.

The phenomenon of sound is in itself an inspiration for architecture—or, to an even greater degree, sound creates space. We chose to use sound to recreate and define both the AAC and the installation space. Rather than using a membrane, we introduced the given AAC material as a soft solid. A sound composer was invited to create, or **SAMPLE**, sound bites specific to the gallery. These sound bites were thought of as space generators or deformers, and once imported in Maya, a generative animation software, they were translated into frequencies, or forces. Two generic cylindrical volumes were placed in virtual space; the software enabled the frequencies to scan, deflect, and transform the soft solid's surface into a recorded/recording surface of the sound bites. The two soft solids (endearingly termed "slim" and "fatty" by the builders) span floor-to-ceiling, thus revealing the sets of voids surrounding them, to be read as soundscapes. The resulting **SYNAESTHETIC SPACE** is an

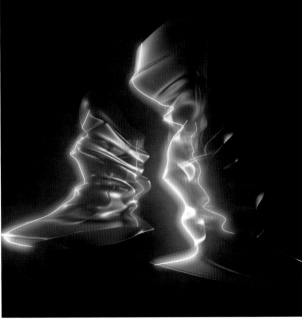

experience of multiple sensory effects, overlapping sound zones, at once physical, visual, and meditative. The ear informs the eye and the eye informs the ear.

In the "real" built environment of the museum, the transformed soft solids are once again scanned by the same sound waves now projected by special automated rotating speakers developed by Robotics International. The speakers slowly trace the forms, transmitting scrambled sound waves, which reorganize upon hitting a surface—the surface becomes the transmitter. Sounds are deflected from the already mutated shape and are reflected at unexpected angles. Subsequently the transmitting soft solid creates an environment of ever-changing three-dimensional sound-scapes. Sound tubes, or vectorial pathways, pass through the solid, not only projecting but also accelerating sound waves in the center space—an auditory corridor can be heard at specific compression zones in the installation. It metamorphoses into a hybrid environment of sound bites, light ripples, and silence—an interactive experience for the visitor who, while moving through the space, will never make the same trip twice.

SOFT SOLID Using this light, easily formed and transformed material, AAC, allowed us to mold these monumental, yet malleable, structures—these soft solids.

Light architecture in the past has often been inspired by the use of music or sound. Two great examples are the Bra installation by Vito Acconci and the Philips Pavilion by Le Corbusier (left).

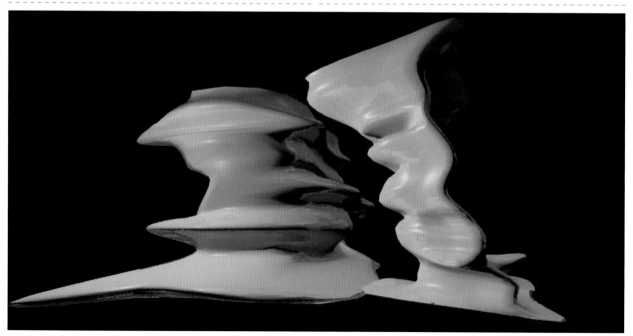

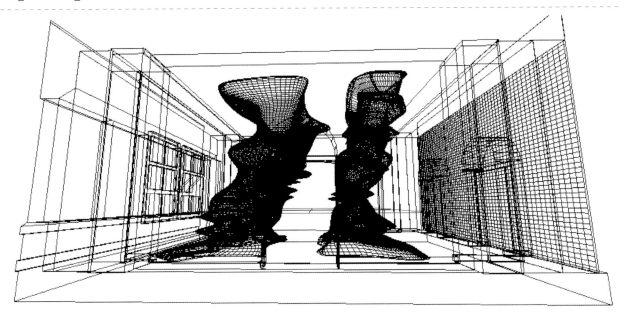

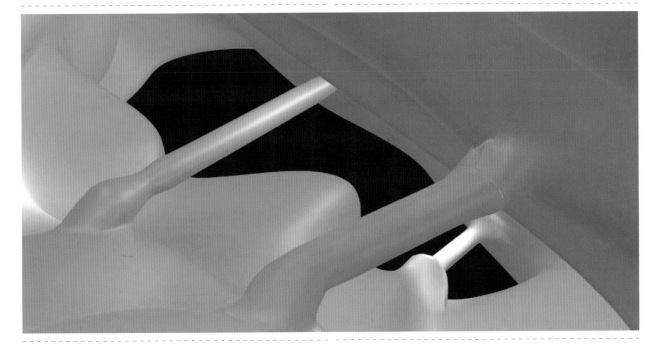

SYNAESTHETIC SPACE The space that surrounds the objects, rather than the objects themselves, creates the soundscape: an acoustic space that examines and exhibits qualities of sound in its pure unfolded form.

SYN-ES-THE-SIA or synaesthesia n **1.** The feeling of sensation in one part of the body when another part is stimulated; **2.** The evocation of one kind of sense impression when another sense is stimulated, for example, the sensation of color when a sound is heard; **3.** In literature, the description of one kind of sense perception using words that describe another kind of sense perception, as in the phrase "shining metallic words"

—*Encarta World English Dictionary*, s.v. "Synesthesia."

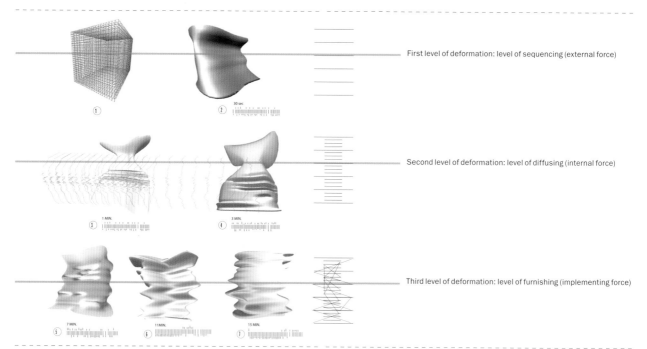

First level of deformation: level of sequencing (external force)

Second level of deformation: level of diffusing (internal force)

Third level of deformation: level of furnishing (implementing force)

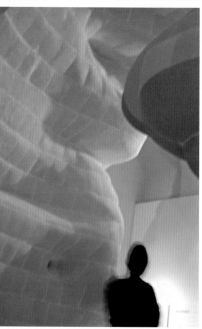

... soundscape_

Sound tubes are inserted in
right angles with the rotating
sound waves to create a special
soundscape between the two soft
solids. Children pick up on this
fast and attempt to accelerate
the effect in multiple ways.

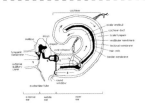

Sound frequencies were translated in Maya into forces to
transform the basic volumes
into "soft solids."

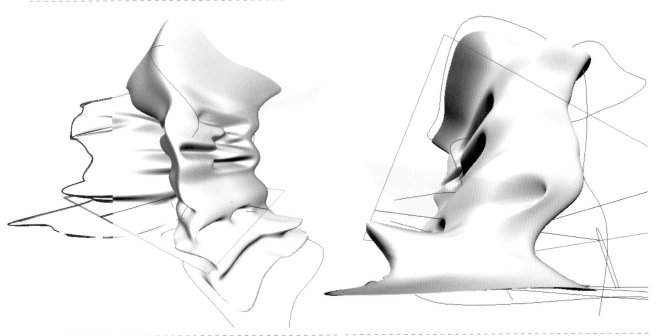

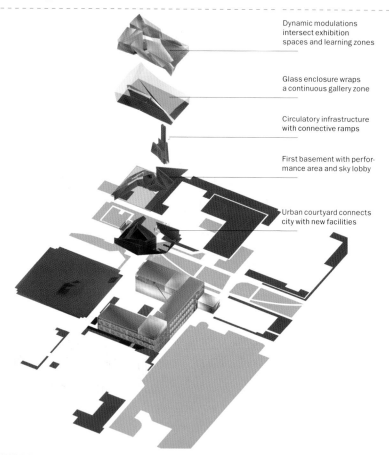

Dynamic modulations
intersect exhibition
spaces and learning zones

Glass enclosure wraps
a continuous gallery zone

Circulatory infrastructure
with connective ramps

First basement with performance area and sky lobby

Urban courtyard connects
city with new facilities

Type	Museum of Art and Design; competition
Location	San Jose State University, San Jose, California
Area	35,329 sq. ft.
Year	2003

San Jose Para-building

The museum extension for San Jose State University's School of Art and Design is based on the concept of a **PARA-BUILDING**. Both supporting and supported by its host, the museum addition further stimulates and activates the operations and functions of the school while providing a more public cultural layer. Designed as an integrated structure, the museum's large C-shaped form wraps from under the existing courtyard, along the school building, and cantilevers back over the courtyard, to create a fluid line of facilities and galleries and an open public entry zone in the now-covered yard. The cantilever casts a welcome shaded area in the square during the hot summer months, while its platform above lifts over the existing structures to provide the visitor with panoramic views of the city and the surrounding mountains.

TOPOLOGICAL BANDS continuously connect the new programs as they move under, up, through, and over the existing structure. Part of the topology folds up, creating a large ramp that extends from the auditorium situated below ground to the elevated museum, passing through the courtyard. The primary entrance to the museum is thus located in the glass lobby of the main building and over the courtyard ramp. The urban court accommodates performances, lunch breaks, and general resting areas. Seating in the form of permanent sculptural elements is a continuation of the topological bands, constructed of various natural textures of wood, stone, and rubber. The courtyard creates both a filter and entry zone for the school and the museum.

The programmatic modulations, as they follow the topology of the bands wrapping and winding up, fluidly link the exhibition spaces, classrooms, offices, and graphic workshops, generate new connections, and stimulate cultural exchange. The bands facilitate integrated exhibition surfaces and built-in furniture, both operating on micro and macro scales. Physically and visually, connectedness is typical throughout this para-building. Green roofs and terraces act as elevated outdoor areas, which are part of the museum's modulations as they circle up to provide light and air to the exhibition spaces.

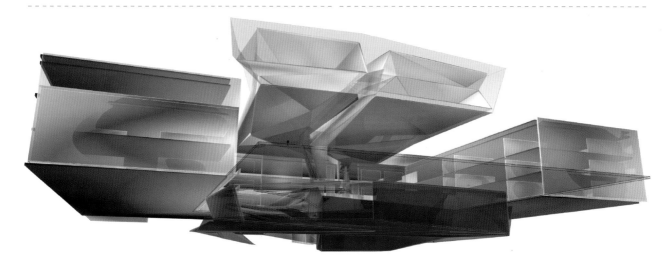

PARA-BUILDING The University's new museum insertion is conceived as a large C-shape wrapping in and around the existing art school, at once an addition and integration—a parabiosis, rather than a parasite.

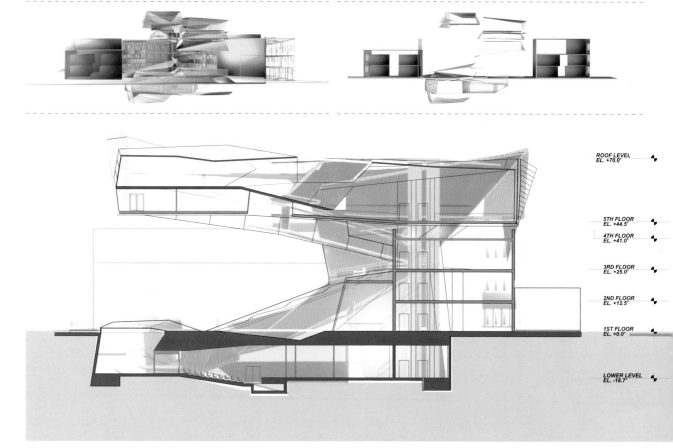

ROOF LEVEL
EL. +70.0'

5TH FLOOR
EL. +44.5'

4TH FLOOR
EL. +41.0'

3RD FLOOR
EL. +25.0'

2ND FLOOR
EL. +12.5'

1ST FLOOR
EL. +0.0'

LOWER LEVEL
EL. -18.7'

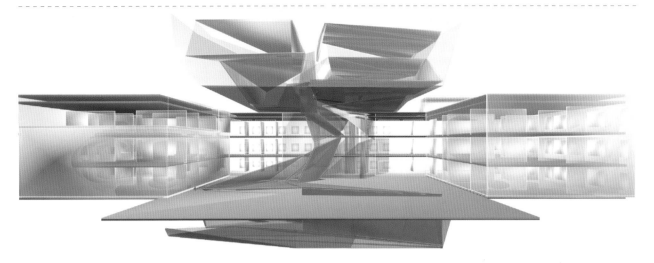

TOPOLOGICAL BANDS Encoded with programs, topological bands fluidly fold up and through the school to connect the education and exhibition of art in multiple ways.

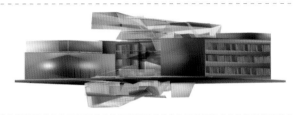

The bands not only programmatically intertwine the university and the cultural areas of the museum, but also create outdoor green spaces and roof gardens for gathering and reflection.

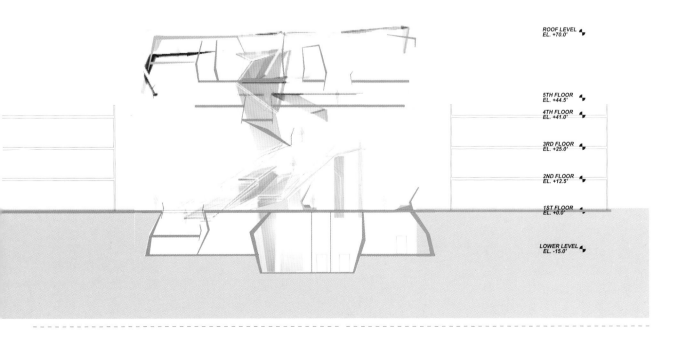

ROOF LEVEL
EL. +70.0'

5TH FLOOR
EL. +44.5'

4TH FLOOR
EL. +41.0'

3RD FLOOR
EL. +25.0'

2ND FLOOR
EL. +12.5'

1ST FLOOR
EL. +0.0'

LOWER LEVEL
EL. -15.0'

The strenuous, tight structural lines of the insertion give clear vectorial sightlines and fluid spatial connectors. The space acts as an urban and academic cultural attractor. As the volume cantilevers over the courtyard, it creates a filter space—a soft transition from the exterior to the interior.

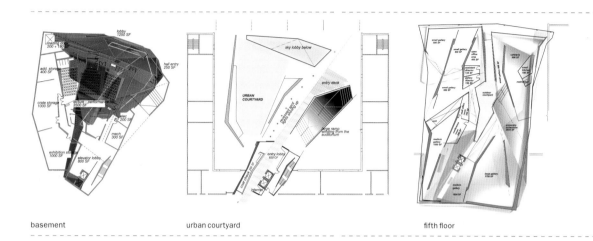

basement   urban courtyard   fifth floor

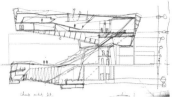

Programmatic fluidity was calculated in an indexical diagram, illustrating different options for the integration of educational and museum programs.

BASEMENT (B)

B-1	B-2	B-3	B-4	B-5	B-6	B-7	B-8	B-9	
Exhibition Storage 1000 sq. ft.	Crate Storage 1000 sq. ft.	Storage 400 sq. ft.	Hall Entry 500 sq. ft.	Loading Dock 200 sq. ft.	Sky Lobby 1200 sq. ft.	Mechanical 300 sq. ft.	Electrical 200 sq. ft.	Elevator Lobby 800 sq. ft.	5600 sq. ft.

ENTRY/ URBAN COURTYARD (E)

E-1	E-2	E-3	E-4	E-5	
Entry Lobby 820 sq. ft.	Coat Check 250 sq. ft.	Security 250 sq. ft.	Urban Courtyard 4200 sq. ft.	Internet 60 sq. ft.	5580 sq. ft.

THIRD/FOURTH FLOOR (3/4)

3/4-1	3/4-2	3/4-3	3/4-4	3/4-5	3/4-6	3/4-7	3/4-8	3/4B-9	
Classroom 1 1100 sq. ft.	Classroom 2 1100 sq. ft.	Orientation 550 sq. ft.	Archives 1000 sq. ft.	Dirty Area 250 sq. ft.	Clean Area 250 sq. ft.	Graphics Prep. 250 sq. ft.			4500 sq. ft.

FIFTH FLOOR (5)

5-1	5-2	5-3	5-4	5-5	5-6	5-7	5-8	5-9	
Cafe 190 sq. ft.	Small Gallery 1 500 sq. ft.	Small gallery 2 500 sq. ft.	Small Gallery 3 500 sq. ft.	Small Gallery 4 500 sq. ft.	Small Gallery 5 500 sq. ft.	Open Office Area 400 sq. ft.	Gallery Director 150 sq. ft.		4500 sq. ft.

5-10	5-12	5-13	5-14	5-15	5-16	
Director's assistance 125 sq. ft.	Conference Room 250 sq. ft.	Large gallery 1 1750 sq. ft.	Large Gallery 2 1750 sq. ft.	Medium Gallery 1 1000 sq. ft.	Medium Gallery 2 1000 sq. ft.	7365 sq. ft.

Type   Retail/office;
          invited competition
Location New York City
Area   12,000 sq. ft.
Year   2000

INVERSION The flagship store is located in an existing cast-iron building in Tribeca. It is an inverted space; the ground floor continues down two floors below the street surface. The three-story headquarters will be spatially and virtually connected through the insertion of nomadic structures, mediating bodies.

FILTER SPACE A translucent light zone cuts into the existing floor with a set of metal floor grilles, stairs, and recessed light fixtures, creating a filter space—an animated environment of light and shadow—that connects the inverted space.

Issey Miyake Flagship Store

"I want you to give me the freedom of watching you. Just watching. I am just asking you to let me watch from a corner like this. When you get used to me, I'll be just like the waste basket." He shifted his position to the tip of the isosceles triangle whose base formed the line connecting her with me. Fish, birds, animals—all engage in strange courtship ceremonies before mating. According to specialists, it's apparently a modified form of attack and threat.
—Kobo Abe, *The Box Man*

The location for the new Issey Miyake Flagship Store is in the fashionable Tribeca district. The existing street-level space contains the majority of its area below ground—a true feature of New York City. The three-story inverted store submerges itself in the city, a top-down space for a bottom-up organization. The design expresses this **INVERSION**, envisioned here as "suspension." Mediating spatial volumes are suspended between floors, stretching beyond the traditional boundaries of the space to create ambiguity and blur defined edges.

The ground floor acts as an urban destination that contains several temporal programs. The conference room is situated halfway between the first and second floors, while the press room, its inverted partner, creates an additional glass volume in the first basement, at once connecting and dividing. An open office area, adjacent to the press room, is located just below the filtered glass sidewalk. Luminous dividers create privacy between the workstations while maintaining spatial continuity. Suspended below the back skylight, corrugated cardboard cocoons form fitting rooms, and translucent display

volumes inserted in the front and side facades transfix delicate fashion pieces between interiority and urban exteriority. Additional metal grilles are introduced into the floors, and stairs and platforms of metal grating allow the light to **FILTER** through all three levels. This new fashion landscape celebrates its inverted quality by suspending **BODIES** in space thus guiding light into its deeper levels. A palette of materials, such as aluminum honeycombs and etched fiberglass, combined with cardboard and concrete corrugations, metal grating, and dividers that contain and distribute light, produce an omnipresent glow and mark nearby forms and volumes with lines of shadow and light.

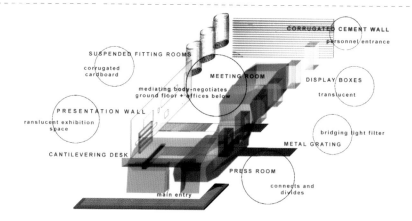

A section through the new flagship store reveals the suspended meeting rooms, made out of a translucent fiberglass construction.

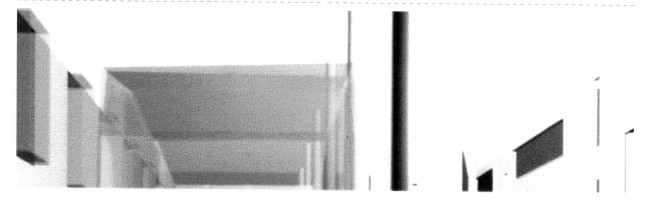

MEDIATING BODIES Miyake's fashion research incorporates nomadic shapes and innovative materials. Here, the space induces a sense of temporality through the insertion of suspended fitting "cocoons" of recycled cardboard, translucent suspended meeting rooms, and transparent exhibition volumes that negotiate the street facade.

Type	Residential
Location	New York City
Area	5,000 sq. ft.
Year	1998

PIVOT POINT A freestanding bathroom capsule forms the pivotal point around which the public and private zones of the loft reorganize. Fields of occupation are generated with continuous space flowing between them. This results in a more fluid domestic environment with integral amenities—defeating the traditional hallway/room configuration.

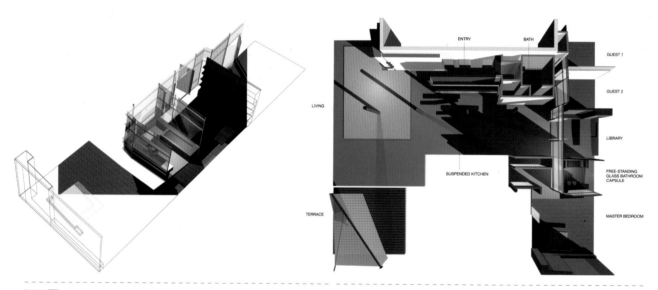

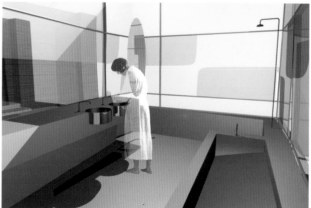

Wooster Street Loft

It is not the conduct of bodies but rather the conduct of something that existed between them, i.e. the field, that could be essential for ordering and interpreting all events.
—Albert Einstein

The nomadic quality of today's metropolitan life and a temporal urban living condition are the premise for the design of the Wooster Street Loft, a 5,000-square-foot raw space in SoHo. As a part-time housing unit, the loft offers an opportunity to reflect on urban islands as electronic links that connect physically detached places: as the owner moves between London and New York, the Internet is his primary mode of communication.

In the design for the loft, different zones are generated—public, private, and guest areas. Here, the concept of "**CONNECTIVE CUTS**" is developed to produce continuity in separation. Rather than the traditional configuration of hallways and rooms, programs overlap. The wall-as-barricade that formerly operated between public and private space as a protection device has mutated and remade itself into an interactive membrane, a crease that allows for slippage, leakage, and errors. Mistakes then become active ingredients in a series of displacements and replacements, constantly diverting the real. The space is composed of intersections of pivoting, adaptable elements and is shaped by operations that orient, situate, temporalize, and make each component function in a polyvalent unity of conflictual programs or contractual proximities.

A free-floating bathroom capsule is the main **PIVOTING POINT** between public and private areas. Enveloped in a folded glass skin and open to the bedroom area, its functions are sculpted into one continuous blue concrete surface. This meditative space for cleansing both spiritually and physically forms an island of calm in an otherwise hectic urban environment. Such areas act as hinges around which the public and private zones of the loft are negotiated.

The ceiling planes dip down to allow for the subtle encasement of all installations, smoothly meeting the tilted, fragmented vertical planes of capsule-like spaces, such as the bathrooms. Surfaces are introduced as connective membranes not only by means of translucency, but also by slicing and separating these planes into suspended elements. Conventional domestic components are thus transformed. The kitchen functions are integrated within the folds of the entry wall. Two cantilevering planes flank the kitchen area; a fixed concrete work surface hovers over a pivoting translucent custom-poured polyurethane breakfast bar. As the section plane is sliced, one occupies several programmatic zones at the same time.

As a result, areas or fields of occupation—living, dining, and sleeping—have been formed with fluid, continuous space flowing between them. Changes in the **TEXTURES** of the surfaces—walls, floors, and windows—further designate these spaces as hard, soft, and neutral zones. Doors and enclosures are replaced by shifts in volume, and transitions into different areas become hinge-points, while providing visual privacy. Overall, the continuity of these interlocking volumes creates a residence of overlapping intersections and interweaving space—a digital continuum.

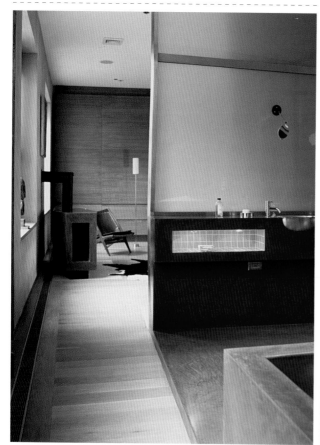

INVERSION The bathing unit is built like an inverted sailboat; here wood ribs are lined with curved plywood and polyester and finished with an intense blue waterproof cement layer to achieve a smooth, solid surface.

SMOOTH TEXTURES Areas are subtly designated by texture changes only; the public areas are finished in cementitious materials with recessed carpets and the private zones are finished with walnut wood floors and walls. All surfaces are flush, only feet register a changing grade of softness.

CONNECTIVE CUTS A kitchen is placed within the fold of a wall section, its work surfaces suspended. As the wall section is sliced, one is within several rooms at once, visually and physically connected. Two large cantilevering countertops are suspended from an existing wood column with a strong steel pivot ring, creating a flexible kitchen area with two pivoting surfaces.

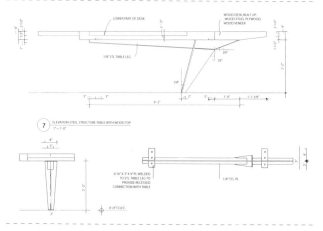

Elements are designed to be transformative; pivoting, suspended, and cantilevering units help constantly transform the spatial reconfiguration.

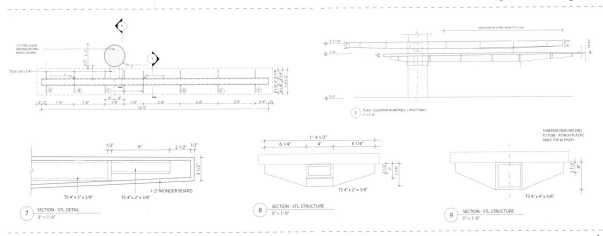

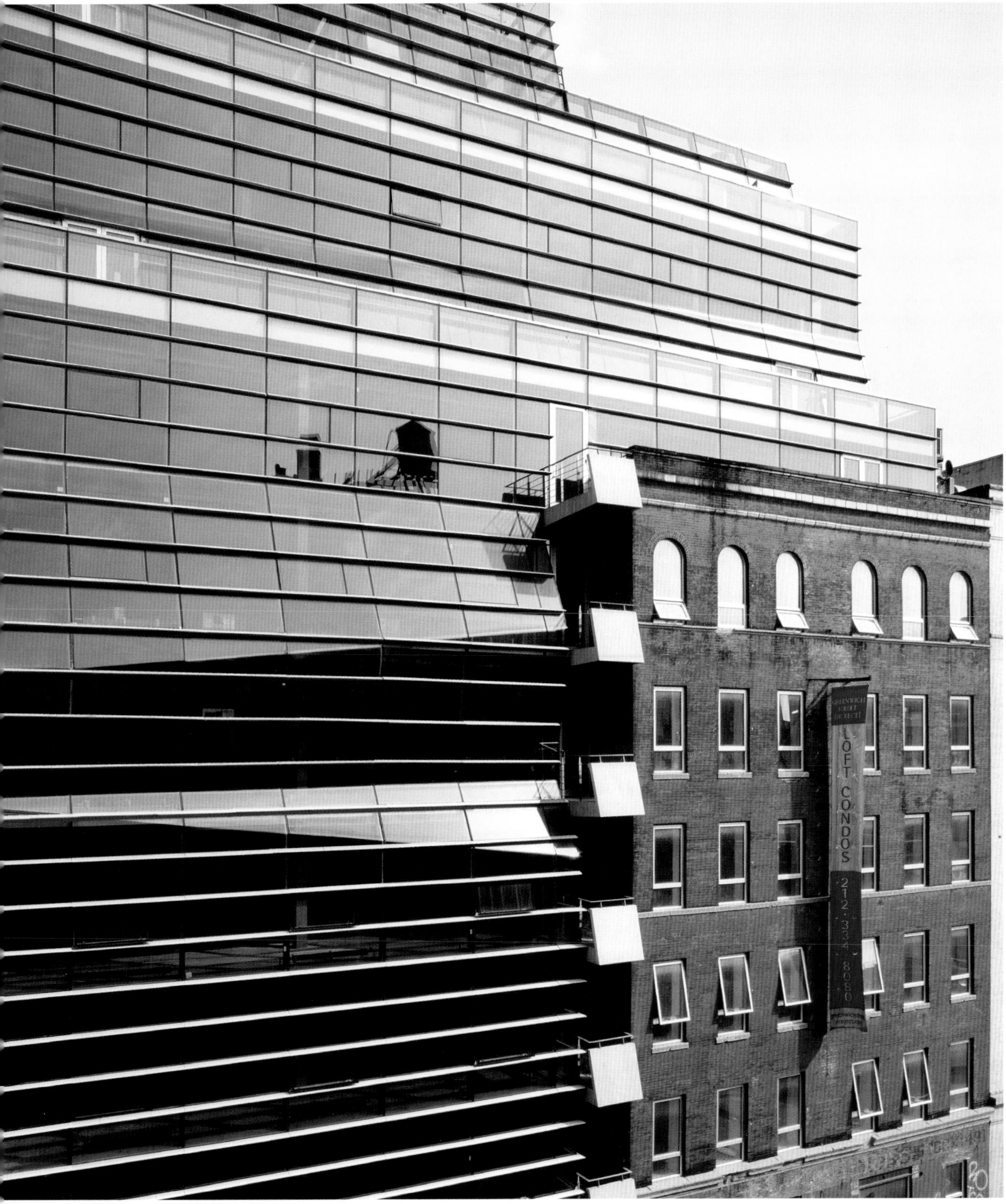
LOFT CONDOS
212·334·8080

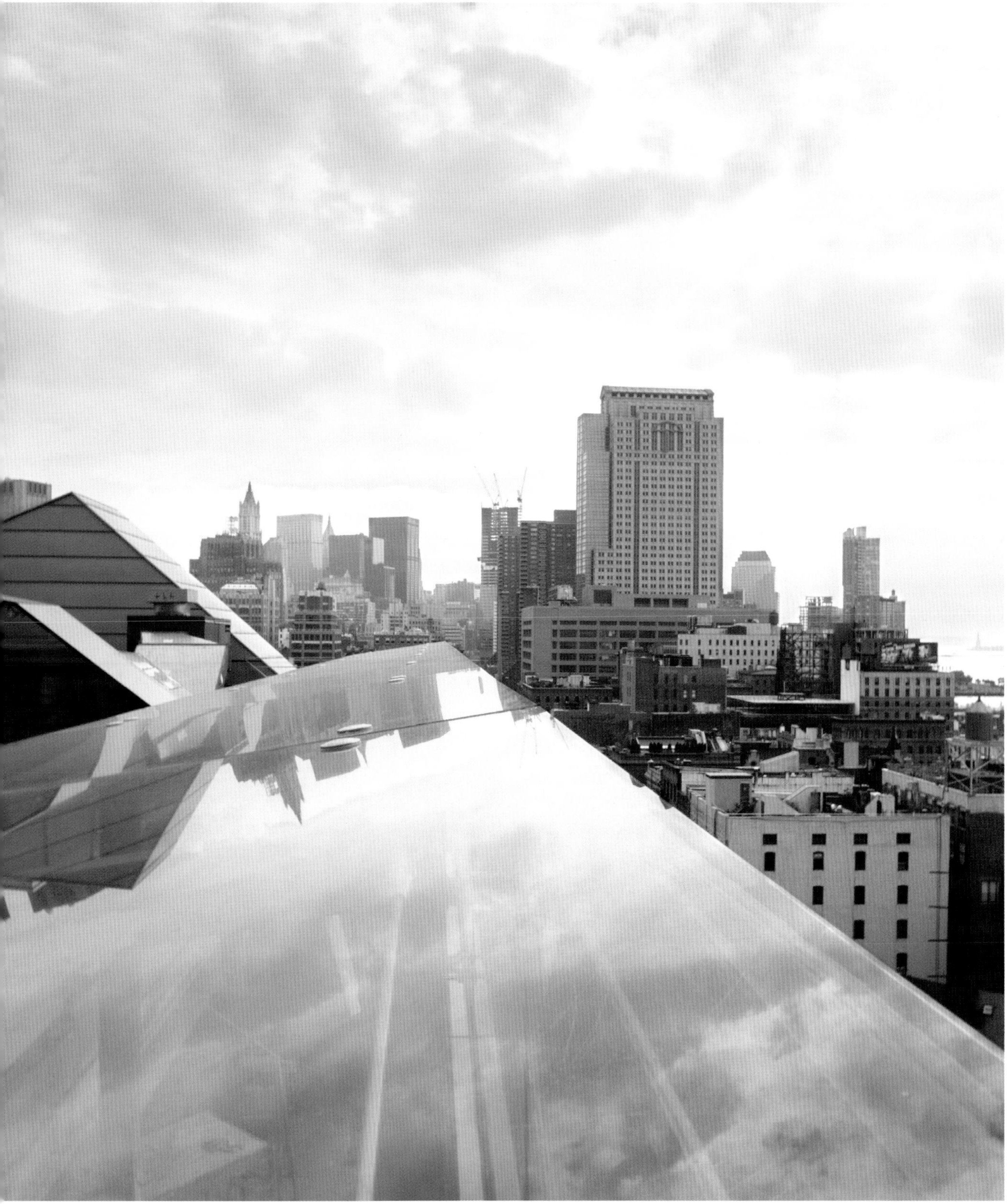

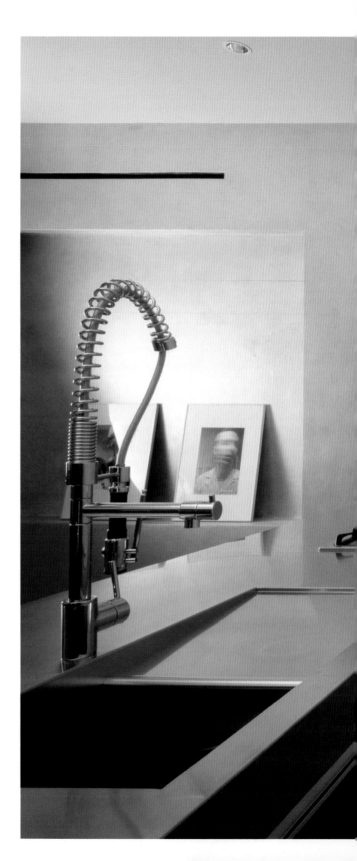

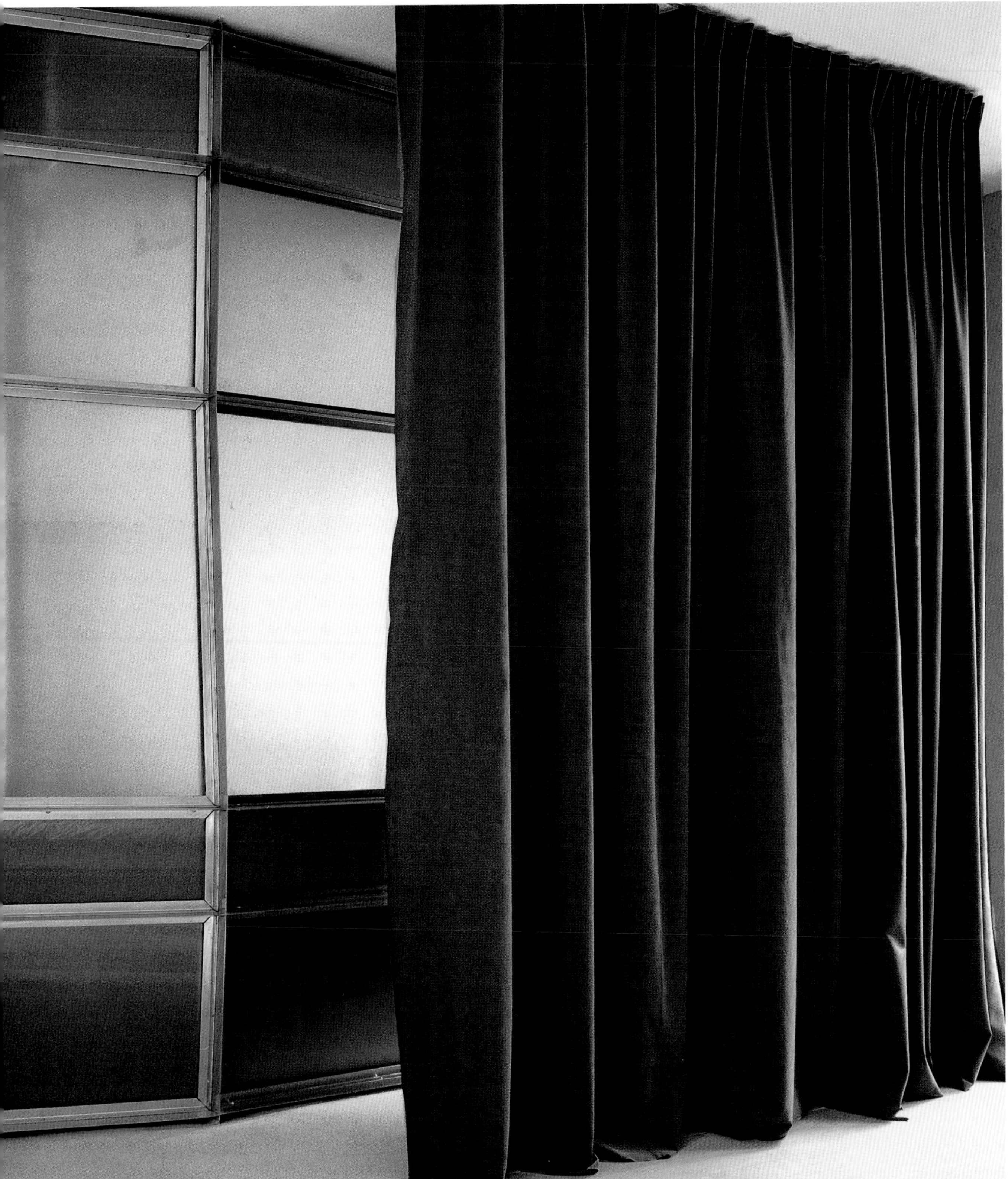

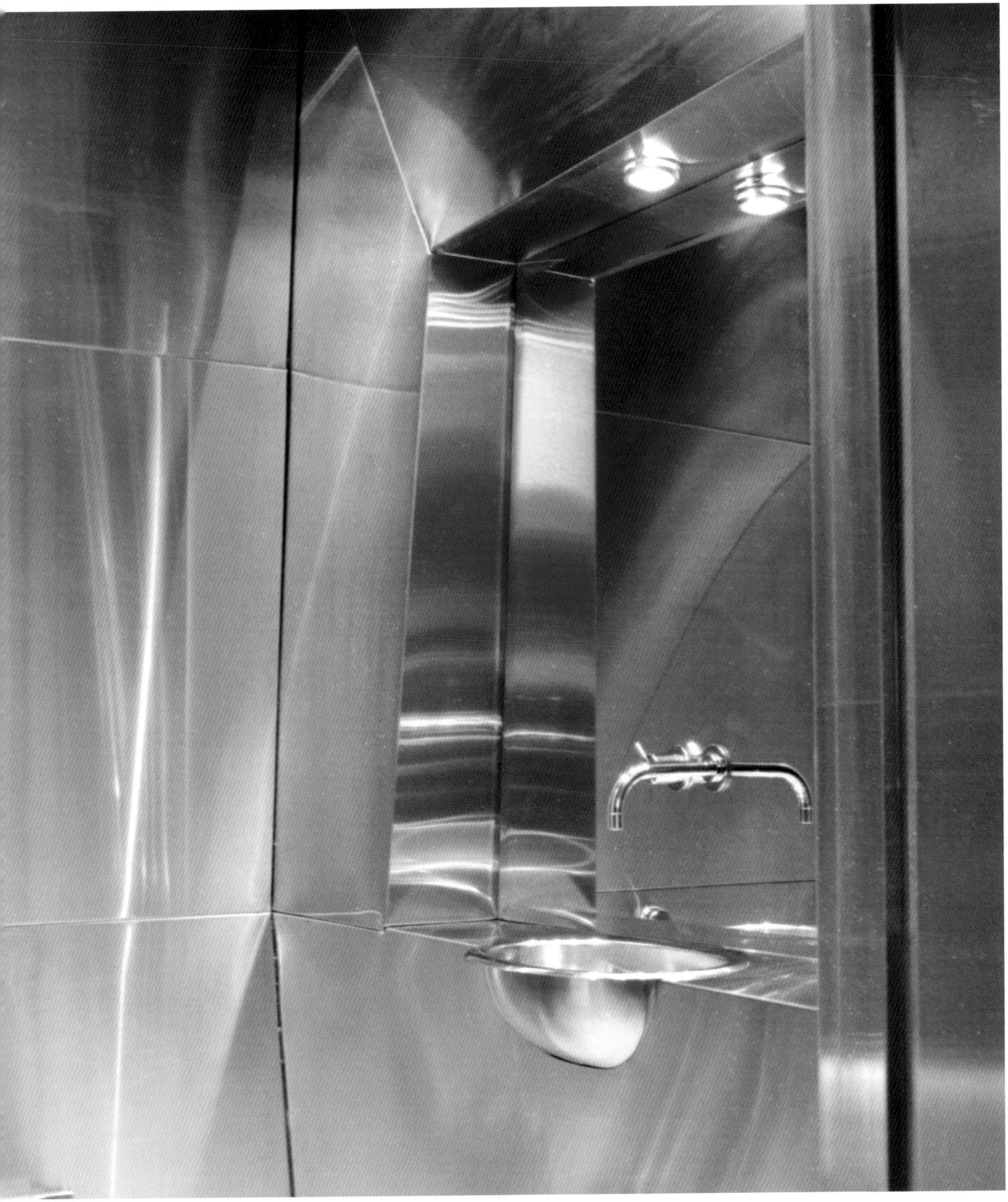

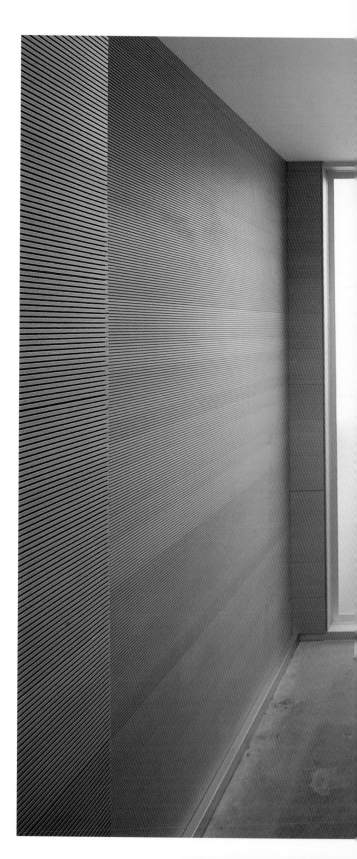

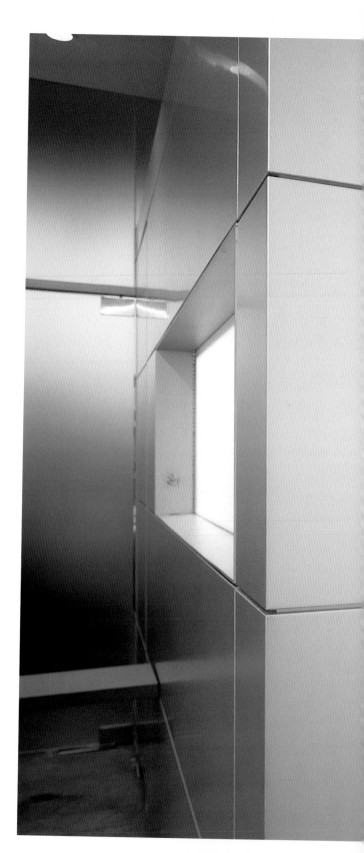

SUR·FACE *n* **1.** the outermost or uppermost part of a thing, the one that is usually presented to the outside world, and can be seen and touched **2.** the part of the Earth, the sea, or any water that meets the atmosphere **3.** a solid flat area, for example, on top of a fitment or piece of furniture, especially an area on which it is suitable to work **4.** a relatively thin outer layer or coating applied to something, usually to give it a smooth finish **5.** the superficial parts or aspects of something, especially when contrasted with the essence of the thing **6.** a flat or curved continuous area definable in two dimensions; *adj* **1.** occurring or used on, or relating to, the surface of something **2.** applying only to the outermost or uppermost part **3.** put on for effect and not natural, deep-seated, or deeply felt **4.** operating or transported over land or sea but not in the air

—*Encarta World English Dictionary*, s.v. "Surface."

surface

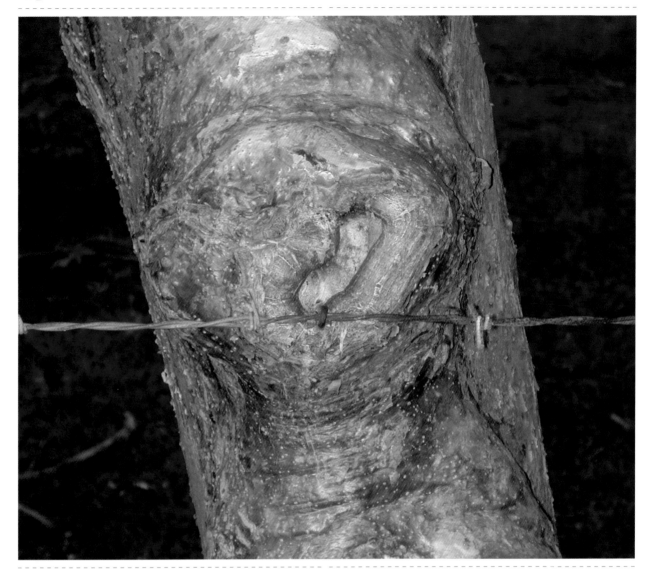

BIOMES are defined as "the world's major communities, classified according to the predominant vegetation and characterized by adaptations of organisms to a particular environment."[1] Over time, biomes have changed and adapted. More recently, human interactions have drastically altered these communities. Their organic flexibility allows for peak performance and, in the worst case, survival.

Shown here, the *Simaruba Clade of Bursera*, or *Papello* (it sheds skin like paper), initially grows with a conventional trunk and self-supporting branches. With age, the branches grow back on themselves. When irritated, the bark of the outer skin reacts, creating extra skin texture, or callous, that protects the tree from the irritant and results in a wild abundance of growth variations.

This organic structure, as expressed in a recording of behavioral processes through a series of surface deflections, gains intelligence and transforms the system as a whole. Similar to Edmund Husserl's "thing-shapes," which find specificity through their relationship to the human body in their surfaces—"more or less smooth, more or less perfect"—these registrations strive for gradual perfection.[2] This striving allows variation to emerge. The surfaces mutate in a system of recordings—the politics of layering, creasing, and wrapping activate zones and environments where boundaries are negotiated and distinctions are blurred. This mutation conflates mathematical behavior with industrial precision into a set of smart layers and hybrid structures.

[1] Stephanie Pullen, ed., "The World of Biomes," University of California, Berkeley, http://www.ucmp.berkeley.edu/glossary/gloss5/biome.
[2] *Edmund Husserl's The Origin of Geometry*, introduction by Jacques Derrida (Lincoln, NE: University of Nebraska, 1962).

Process is More Important than Form*

A Conversation with Winka Dubbeldam
Javier Barreiro Cavestany

In recent years architectural discourse has turned around "skins," "folds," and "fissures," the aesthetic and philosophic corollaries of which have surface as an emblem. Thus, attribute is turned into substance. This enthronement of appearance finds its analogy in the mask, a fact consistent with an age ruled by the image in its most ephemeral sense: the look. An idea reflected at the antipodes of the canons of antiquity—for the Greeks, the mask was the essence of what is real, a concentrate of character and its truth.

Much of postmodern culture has wished to formulate an epistemology on the basis of the dissolution of dogmas and certainties, resulting in a sort of quantism that would justify the "anything goes" attitude of the tribal-global present. Thus, the idea of an "intelligent" surface wavers between being a functional instrument and the search for—and defense of—pure form as the last bastion of aestheticism, betraying a longing for a past when form knew its content.

The poetics (or politics?) of skins and folds imply a mutable architecture, in which the relationship between profile and structure, between core and epidermis, tends to become blurred. Winka Dubbeldam has developed this dialectic by calling for a "generative architecture focused on performance rather than form," so that walls and facades cease to be dividing elements and become connecting tissues. Something exemplified by (or derived from) her works, which go from the skeleton and its articulations to the juxtaposition of not yet wholly crystallized forms; a dynamic that exposes the interiority of the organism by means of a functional gesture charged with meaning.

Therein lies the guiding thread of Dubbeldam's praxis, in the ambit of design and construction as well as in the dynamic synthesis of the exhibition From HardWare to SoftForm, in whose images structural elements cease to be the supports of appearance and take on autonomous expressive valences—a vocabulary (and a syntax) of hypermodern morphology, which paradoxically alludes to fossils or stylized prototypes of vaguely Jurassic beings.

In line with this evolutionary analogy, Dubbeldam's treatment of forms and materials derives from the logic of bricolage as formulated by biologists such as Jacob and Monod, in which each organism is the product of an assemblage of heteroclite objects found in situ and also a response to chance—and yet necessary—challenges and stimuli, whose inter-action with the context recurs to different strategies: from assimilation through contrast to the alien presence that establishes a new balance in the territory.

This stripping away of appearances shows how, in the interplay of desire and represen-tation, stratifications and wrappings make it possible to annul the rigid dichotomies of subject/object or exterior/interior in favor of juxtapositions and shiftings that redefine the relations between architecture and context, public and private, function and user. This poses the critical issue of architecture as object or architecture as process; a dilemma that involves the user in a double critical role: as protagonist of a cognitive-spatial experience or as a mere "living" object subjected to a geometrical logic.

In the metaphorical equation of ethics/aesthetics a "multidimensional" factor recurs, capable of integrating elasticity and rigidity, form and function, in order to accommodate collective needs and individual desires as part of a reflection on new frontiers and territo-ries of architecture. Some of these issues were discussed in a conversation with Winka Dubbeldam in Mexico City in March 2003.

Cavestany: Could we establish a similar relationship—as the one between inner and external image—in the passage from virtual to physical dimension of space? I would like you to consider this process in the different aspects of your work: projects, installations, constructions. **Dubbeldam:** In an exhibition I don't want to represent a duplicate of a project to show it in a museum. If people want to see my built work, they can go and see the real thing. When I did the show From *Hard*Ware to Soft*Form*, I thought that it was an opportunity for further research beyond the material construction because a building has a series of restrictions, which I actually do like when I am building. The great thing about an exhibition is the possibility to think about the conceptual reading of a house in another dimension, and the different interactions that people can have with that concept. So in this installa-tion the visitors cause the deflection or transformation of the images. Starting with the computer, the visitors give feedback through an interactive floor, which in turn instigates projections of the images in space. This dynamic relationship between the human body and the organic part of architecture is like an armature or a kind of space that I call "phoro-nomic"—a gradual approximation that becomes itself generative of new spaces. The result is never perfect, I hate perfection. I think perfection is boring. Instead, there is something beautiful about accident, when things never completely fit. **Cavestany:** Does this relate to the difference between architecture as object and architecture as experience? **Dubbeldam:** Yes. The whole idea of the installation was in that tension between object and environment. The point was in neither of the two, but in every phase in between. The environment has to do with the process of becoming something; the object, with the idea of generating something else. This is the ultimate goal. **Cavestany:** Isn't there a risk of turning the user of a building into an object within an another object? **Dubbeldam:** I can give you an example. My clients for the GT Residence are a couple; she works in the art world and he is an insurance agent, the most pragmatic person. He was primarily interested in the size of the garage and in the storage spaces. Now that it's finished, he seems to be more interested in the architecture. He understands that the structure creates the possibility of turning space inside out—the inner part of the house contains more light, and the skylight which turns into wall completely pulls nature into its center. The shape regresses and becomes calmer, and the actual spatial experience of the lightness in the center interacts strongly with the landscape while the rest of the space acts as a lounging void that releases tension toward the outside—the "object becomes environment." There isn't much force or violence in the space, so it becomes meditative and reflective, in an almost zen way. That's why I think that the essence of my architecture is hard to photograph. It's more suited to being filmed. **Cavestany:** Within the specific features of each project, could you tell what is at present truly new in the relationship between space and user? **Dubbeldam:** In terms of dwelling architecture, I think that the traditional home was very hierarchical, with a rigid division between public and private space. This division has faded, there are overlapping zones created by shifting certain elements that change the configuration of the space, not as a static device but in a dynamic way, eliminating all rigid boundaries: the whole house can turn into a living room or become a series of private areas without connections between them. This leads us to rethink what is public and what is private, and questions: how far do you want the others to go into your privacy? **Cavestany:** To what extent are people aware of their needs and desires in terms of space? **Dubbeldam:** Clients are more involved in choosing tiles or colors than in what structure or sense space they want. Initially the budget and basic functional requirements are discussed. Most of the time clients choose an architect because they have seen his/her work. So it's up to you to come up with an idea that fits needs unknown to the client. In this house, the idea came from the fact that when I grew up, we were often on vacation. My father didn't like working, so he concentrated his work in very short periods and then we would make long travels. What I love about vacation houses is the lack of hierarchy, that's why you feel so comfortable. There is no real separation between public and private spaces, there is a fluid inside-outside connection. In this house you can go from the dinning room to the kitchen to the bedroom, or enter any of them through the terrace, a subset of interlocking zones rather than the hierarchical relationship between hallways and rooms. So there is constant access, both from the outside and the inside, to all the spaces in the house. **Cavestany:** What role does the context play in the conception of a project, not only in terms of landscape or of a preexisting urban reality, but in a cultural sense? **Dubbeldam:** I am interested in the politics of space. Not only between urban code and personal will, but in terms of how you negotiate boundaries and blur or dissolve them. In the building on Greenwich Street in New York, we wanted to preserve a continuous urban fabric, so we restored the old building to respect the predominant industrial type of facade while wrapping a new structure over it. So it became like keying into it rather than superimposing. But there is also a political side (which I guess is very Dutch) in a certain democratic use of space, in trying to appropriate something without possessing it. That's why the building has cantilevered balconies sitting along the neighbor's side, which may seem politically incorrect. The same happens on the front, where the building hangs over the street, as a negotiation of the private and the public. What we tried to introduce is something very uncommon in New York: private exterior spaces.

We have talked mainly about residential issues, but in commercial spaces there is a much larger flexibility between public and private, because you can really pull in urban sites or activities. And clients often want it. Another thing is how you treat hierarchies between managing directors and the personnel. It's a kind of struggle between top and bottom users, because you are dealing with power issues. I am kind of manipulative in that sense; I attempt to dissolve these hierarchies, but I try to slip this in an apparently casual way. I am interested in how far you can change attitudes by changing rules and codes of behavior through architecture. **Cavestany:** This takes us back to the beginning, but introducing another element: emotion. That is, instead of the relationship between inner and external gaze, the one between inner emotion and external shape while answering to the functions requested by the client. How does this process work? **Dubbeldam:** Mathematical simulations are beautiful not because mathematicians want to make them beautiful, but because the transformations of a structure bear a certain beauty linked to necessity, not to aesthetics. So when we started working on From *Hard*Ware to Soft*Form*, the simulations of a series of transformations of structures were not based on preconceived forms. We started slicing the objects (which is what mathematicians usually do to analyze a complex form) and writing scripts to animate them. The role of emotion came later, when I realized that there was something endearing about these animations. We were doing research in binary terms through programming, when the structures crystallized in that kind of skeletons with zoomorphic, even human, shapes. Only then did I think of giving them names, reflecting certain emotions, or relationships to the viewer. **Cavestany:** This concerns the images of the exhibition, but when you work on a project to be built, I guess there is an initial shape (or series of shapes) linked to the program. What role does emotion play in the development of this shape? **Dubbeldam:** Materials and scale are very important. I tend to wrap things tightly for intensely private spaces, its privacy expressed both in a change in scale and texture, and then I let spaces go until they release their energy. I love the tension between something small and very private, and more neutral fields unwrapping from those, not unlike the process by which a certain turbulence rises until I can manage to calm things down in a sort of lake, a neutral playground where I can negotiate the user's needs. I want my spaces to be comfortable. I don't think my clients have to suffer by trying to adapt to my architecture. I don't want to be a dictator of space.

This interview was originally published with a different introduction, *Arquine* 24, Summer 2003.

URBAN FIELD On Greenwich Street, an industrial zone on the west side of Manhattan, a new residential glass building wraps over a renovated six-story warehouse.

GW 497 Lofts

Type	Mixed-use/residential lofts
Location	New York City
Area	77,000 sq. ft.
Year	2000–04

Located on the edge of New York City's SoHo district, a six-story warehouse is renovated with a new eleven-story "smart loft" building that wraps up and over it. The building contains twenty-three residential lofts, generous terraces and balconies, an art gallery, and retail spaces, totaling 77,000 square feet. The integration of the existing construction with the steel and glass structure instigates mediation between past and present and creates an **URBAN CONTINUITY**. In this way the once dilapidated urban condition of abandoned warehouses is reinvigorated with the insertion of retail, culture, and modern living.

By reinterpreting the New York City building code, or **RE-CODING**, a diagonal surface bifurcates the facade, challenging the horizontal plane of traditional urban fabric. The strict building setback regulations are integrated into the folded vertical landscape of the glass facade. The traditional two-dimensional surface transforms into a three-dimensional space, to be occupied and inhabited. Paul Virilio and Claude Parent describe a similar condition in the "Third Urban Order"[1]: "neither the horizontal (the agricultural), nor the vertical (the skyscraper), but an oblique system of planes, moving between these two orientations, is of relevance here." But the crease, or fold of the facade, moves beyond the oblique plane, becoming a multiplicity, an inflection of systems, a generative tool. This modulation—the production of spatial constructs—is no longer a static device but a dynamic set of inflections, not literally moving objects, but surface registrations of force fields, "smart systems," and programmatic mappings. This generative, process-oriented approach is the basis and definition of the organismic paradigm—in which an organism is characterized by its immanent patterns of organization. These internal organizing phenomena occur on all levels: in social interaction, in individual behavioral processes, and in nature.

The crystalline glass zone of the new building merges with the more solid and opaque zones of the existing warehouse. In the narrow **CREASE**, or junction, that rises between the two structures a set of cantilevering balconies juxtaposes and differentiates between the old and the new and the urban and the private; the crease as mediation and the glass inflections as spatial device allow for slippage between interior urbanism and urban privacy. At the ground floor, a sloping concrete ramp folds up to meet the delicate glass surfaces of the suspended awning and curtain wall to a slightly elevated entry platform. The main lobby, art gallery, and retail spaces are all accessible by this concrete terrazzo structure. The elongated entry path filters the more reactive streetscape, easing the

transition of the former industrial area into an integrated residential neighborhood.

The Greenwich Street building's main feature is a fully custom and innovative glass curtain wall, a light suspended waterfall of insulated bent glass panels—the first of its kind. The angled facade was originally conceived as a standard curtain-wall system with a limited amount of mutation, but this proved financially unfeasible for a relatively small building with a modest 10,000-square-foot face. This "problem" presented an opportunity to create a custom-designed, non-standard glass facade, redefining the traditional notion of the curtain wall.

Following a performance-based study, the now **THREE-DIMENSIONAL GLASS ZONE** is freed from a common grid into a system of bands and a layering of horizontal and vertical elements. The differentiation and separation between the facade's vertical structural steel components and the aluminum waterproofing components **OPTIMIZED** its performance and minimized costs and effort. Elegant small steel spacers separate the thin steel verticals from a suspended structure of insulated glass planes and horizontal aluminum fins—floating, folding horizontal bands replace the static grid. Further digital analysis of the curtain-wall structure necessitated bending the actual glass panels in order to guide structural forces smoothly through the facade, thus creating completely transparent folds.

The manufacturing process was economized by folding the glass in Barcelona and extruding the aluminum mullions and fins in Hong Kong (custom-designed to match the exact angles of the facade). Finally, all was assembled in Brooklyn. Installation became the simple action of suspending the glass panels off the folded steel structure, already assembled on site. Electronic communication facilitated the digital transmission of three-dimensional computer drawings between Barcelona, Hong Kong, and Brooklyn, where the manufacturers made all two-dimensional documents, thus minimizing mistakes, and allowing for a fast, efficient manufacturing process. The assembly on site was no longer based on **VIF** (verify in field), but on **VIC** (verify in computer), moving away from a site-oriented to a digital data/computer drawing–based construction method—the site had to adjust to the abstract model, a true revolution for the general contractor.

The new building is constructed as a light steel frame with cantilevering concrete floors, allowing the curtain wall to float off the structure as a real suspended curtain. This combination of glass surfaces and heavy concrete floors provides for

RE-CODE The allowable 85-foot vertical facade inflects on the New York City building code setback of 2.7:1. This inflection resonates through the facade, resulting in a set of oblique planes—an urban interface. This now three-dimensional surface creates a crystalline glass zone to be occupied and inhabited.

CREASE Rising in the crease between the new glass structure and the existing brick facade, a series of cantilevered balconies negotiates an interactive space with the streetscape beyond. The crease as a system of inflections allows for a slippage between interior urbanism and urban privacy.

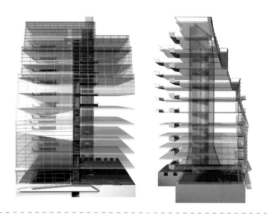

passive solar gain, largely reducing energy use in the winter. The exterior walls, other than the glass wall, are shot-blast gray concrete block with insulated Norwegian windows, a hybrid composition of aluminum and hardwood. All walls and floors are double insulated to create a comfortable living environment with low energy use and high acoustic values.

The twenty-three loft apartments offer an open plan with integrated amenities but no interior divisions. Each loft has been wired for electronic communication, satellite television, and a choice of different heating and cooling systems. The large modern apartments offer an abundance of exterior spaces such as balconies, and roof terraces are situated on both east and west, where residents are able to enjoy the sunsets over the Hudson River from the comfort of their extended living space.

[1] Claude Parent and Paul Virilio, *Architecture Principe: 1966 and 1996* (Paris: Les Editions de l'Imprimeur, 1998).

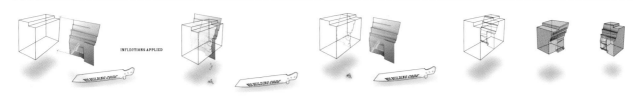

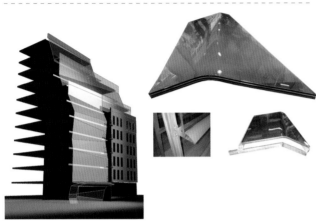

VIF/VIC The three-dimensional digital computer model was electronically transmitted to all manufacturers involved (Barcelona, Hong Kong, and Brooklyn), who then produced the two-dimensional fabrication drawings, guaranteeing exact measurements and fast turnover—transforming the construction process from VIF (verify in field) to VIC (verify in computer).

The fully custom and innovative curtain wall features the separation of structural verticals (ultra-thin steel profiles) and weather proofing horizontals (extruded aluminum fins). The optimization of both structural and waterproofing requirements results in a surprising pattern of diagonal glass folds suspended off a slender set of verticals.

A large frameless glass bulkhead allows private access from the penthouse to the roof terrace. As the curtain wall folds up, it creates a glass parapet, where the glass and the river merge (below).

THREE-DIMENSIONAL GLASS ZONE The custom curtain wall is suspended from the eighth floor and folds out into a frameless glass wing over the entry zone, while at the top of the building it transforms into a glass bulkhead, allowing the building to dissolve in the sky.

At the interior large glass
sliding doors and translucent
surfaces create a flexible
continuous living zone.

For we conceive of human beings as fluctuating between the extreme images that we have categorized as fluctuation and frame, in a sort of back and forth where the simple positions—one, two and three—mark the formal stages in an overall process of individuation. There would thus be a first movement, that of fluctuation towards crystals, where being would be stored in intermediary images as a tendency at most, then following a passage through a frame, there would be a second movement: a turning back where tendency would become a vector, and fluctuation inflection. Such is the pendulum motion of being we wish to describe. —Bernard Cache, *Earth Moves*

MODULATION The Inflection is a dynamic time frame (TW751) extracted from an animated environment; the resultant three-dimensional modulation mediates light and shadow through indirect light. The units organize in clusters to create a secondary datum as a continuity of planar light fields.

Type   Lighting unit for Ivalo
Size   Wall sconce: 23 in.;
            ceiling uplight: 36 in.
Year   2004

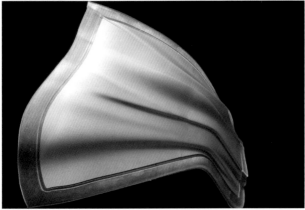 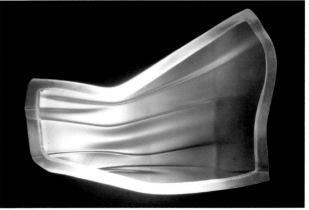

Inflection—TW751

Recently, as we discussed in our studio the influence of industrial design on architecture and were analyzing performance behaviors to generate "intelligent architectures," the unexpected request arrived to design an industrially manufactured product: a light fixture for Ivalo, a young innovative lighting company based in Pennsylvania.

The client, the director of Ivalo, expressed interest in our vision of light as an environment. We proceeded to research this **LIGHTSCAPE** as a spatial effect, rather than as an object. The light as a surface deviation of the ceiling plane allowed us to see the light as a part of a larger system—a crease in the normative. An "animate architecture" is in fact a study of movement and time, here distilled in a lightscape. Contraction, dilation, relativity of movement, and multiplicity describe the "relative" relationship between the two terms.

The TW751, originally a still frame (the 751st frame) of the armature animation investigated in the installation From *Hard*Ware to Soft*Form*, is one of the moments in the transition between object and environment. This virtual moment is a frozen dynamic, a reflection on transformation as an interactive state. As a light environment, it can be organized in clusters to create lightscapes suspended in space. The memory of the ceiling surface as a finite plane is rendered infinite and cloud-like. It combines intersection, fold, and crease, or infinity, line, and space, in one surface.

The TW751 is a sensually folded acrylic plane that fans out to a glowing perimeter. The fixture uses advanced optical waveguide techniques within the acrylic to create an even spread of light around the perimeter of the form. The back of the light is a fluid continuation of the front. When approached from the side in a wall installation, or if seen from above, the sculptural folds/**MODULATIONS** enclose the hardware and attachments in the three-dimensional translucent skin.

Fabrication—These surface manipulations (intersection, fold, crease) are usually found in car or airplane design, where the integration of technologies and built-in intelligence require a supple mold, a perfect fit. The easy fit, the precision mold, and the high-performance model are new and challenging thoughts for an architect, usually indoctrinated by imprecise construction and site conditions. The notion of mass-customization is now rapidly being developed; one orders a custom sneaker online faster than one can walk to the shop. Thus, a heightened level of precision can be introduced in an architecture that hovers between "large furniture" and small buildings. This indefinite state is an exciting new area to be investigated and it begins with the moment that the architect interacts directly with the fabricator, rather than the contractor.

The notation of memories, movement, and time in surface **REGISTRATIONS** of force fields, smart systems, and programmatic mappings create these interactive animate architectures, which thus call into question the permanence of built form and the importance of the relationship between the whole and the part.

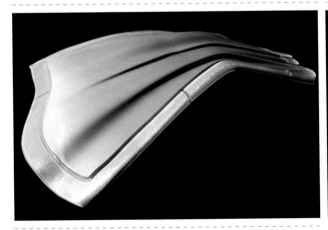

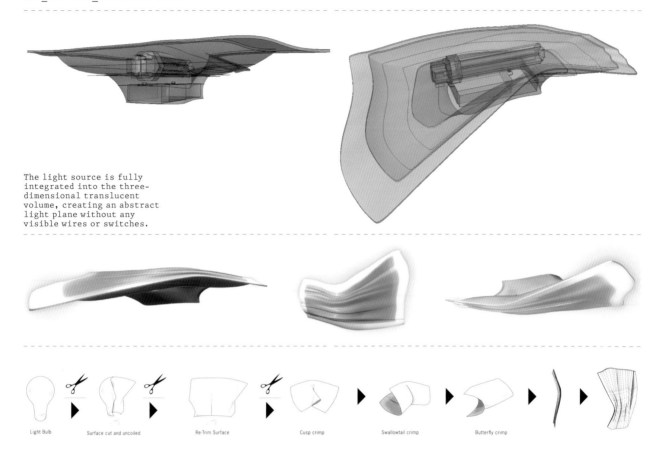

The light source is fully integrated into the three-dimensional translucent volume, creating an abstract light plane without any visible wires or switches.

| Light Bulb | Surface cut and uncoiled | Re-Trim Surface | Cusp crimp | Swallowtail crimp | Butterfly crimp | |

CATASTROPHE THEORY In three-dimensional folding, the fold line takes the form of a curve. The fold itself cannot be collapsed onto a plane. Similarly, the three-dimensional paper folding equivalents of the Cusp, Swallowtail, and Butterfly catastrophes are made up of curved folds and cannot be collapsed onto a flat surface. The origami Cusp fold has one cusp, the Swallowtail two cusps, and the Butterfly three cusps. Intersection, rather than folding, suggests an infinity of continuous planes in space.

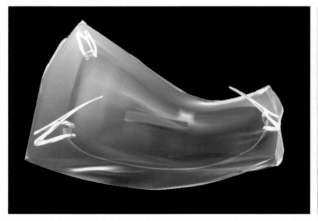

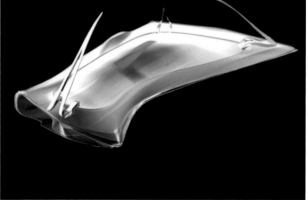

 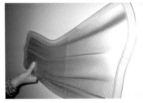

Digital manufacturing/rapid prototyping allows for fast adaptation of test models to investigate light and material effects. As in the airplane wing, the intersection of planes creates tension of form and light reflections.

LIGHTSCAPE The light fixture in clusters creates a lightscape—a plani-sphere (curved segments projected on flat surfaces), a new hovering datum.

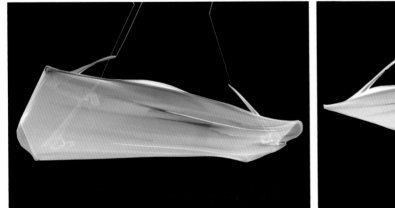 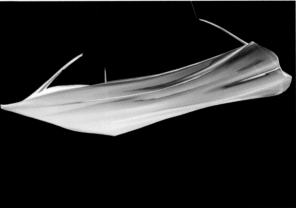

REGISTRATION Memories, movement, and time are etched/registered in the surface through force fields, smart systems, and programmatic mappings to create an interactive animate architecture—the Inflection TW751.

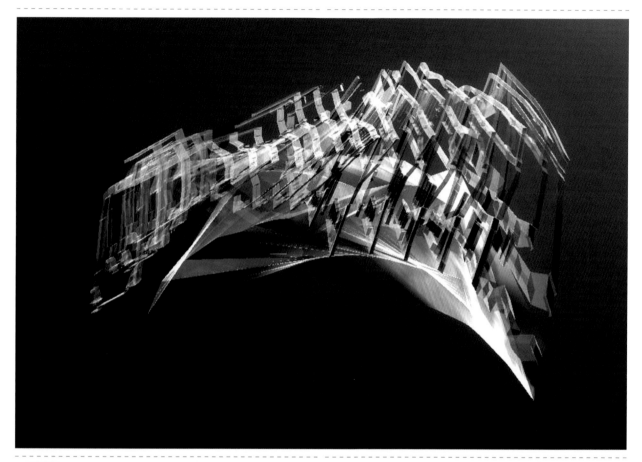

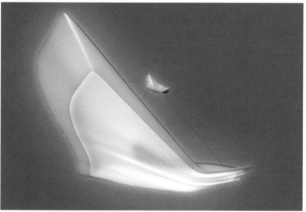

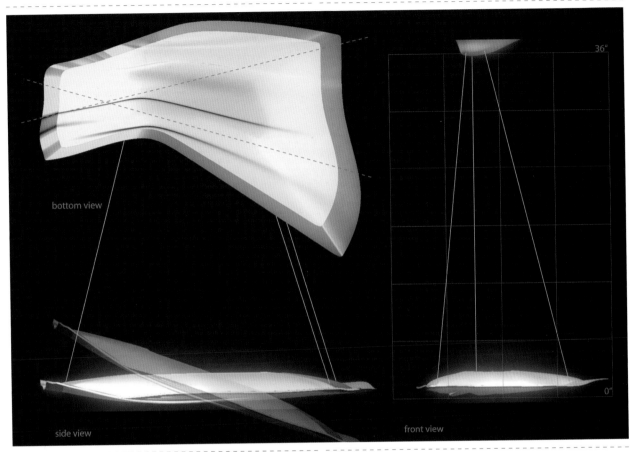

bottom view

side view

front view

36"

0"

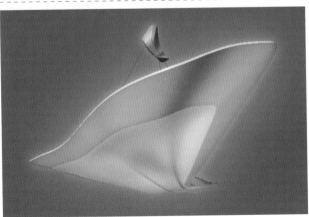

Adjustable ceiling fixtures
are installed alone or in
clusters, creating a swarm of
light surfaces. Angles and
heights are adapted to spatial
and lighting requirements.
The uplight provides indirect
light via the ceiling and adds
an overall glow to the space.

Type	Residential lofts
Location	New York City
Area	32,000 sq. ft.
Year	2004–06

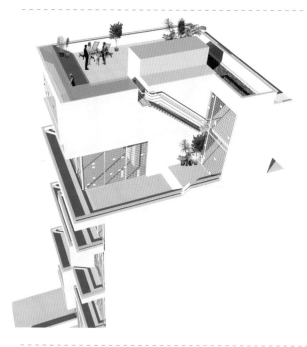

HARD FACE The north facade, an urban street facade, combines stone, translucent stone, and glass in a shifted pattern of translucencies; the stone transforms from opaque during the day to translucent at night.
SOFT SPACE The south facade, a garden facade, provides a set of cantilevering terraces, sunrooms, and balconies, creating its own shadow space—a filter zone to the south sun—while allowing light and views into and out of the units.

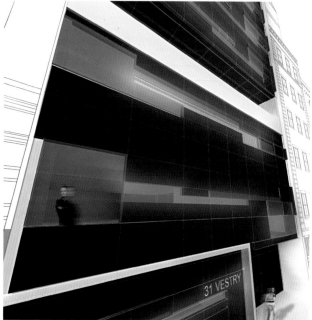

VS 31–33 Lofts

Tribeca's landmark district in New York City, originally a warehouse area, is receiving a new infill. Tired of cheap copies of great old structures, the revered Landmarks Committee has allowed the integration of modern residential buildings into the protected neighborhood. That even the most tradition-valuing institution of the city is excited to see a contemporary modern structure is a long-awaited relief.

Building heights in the area vary greatly. In order to further this differentiation, a tall residential building is designed to occupy a now-abandoned parking lot. Situated between the hard plane of the city fabric and the soft void of the green space behind, the building reacts to urban pressures in a spontaneous way. At the street side (**HARD FACE**), two super-flat stone-composite volumes hover over the sidewalk with glass setback planes interwoven at three levels: the entry, the middle, and the penthouse. In the **SOFT SPACE** of the garden, the building opportunistically pushes out with a series of large transparent cantilevering volumes and planes. These cantilevers contain spacious terraces, suspended living rooms, and areas of shade. Filtered shadow zones fluctuate with the movement of the sun throughout the day and the seasons. These two systems, the projected stone facade at the street and glass volumes at the back, overlap in the center of the

building, causing **SHIFTS** in program and public/private space transitions to occur. Folds in the floor plates further define living zones without separation, maintaining spatial continuity.

These units are considered urban villas rather than lofts because of their extremely generous size (between 3,500 and 5,000 square feet), large outdoor spaces (terraces and gardens), and, often, multiple floors. The interior and exterior spaces flow seamlessly over into each other with continuous surfaces, separated only by clear glass planes. Palatial bathrooms and large bedroom suites create relaxed zones in the residences.

The texture of the hovering stone surfaces at the street side is developed from a fractal-like set of random patterns of glass, strips of laminated glass and stone, and pure stone areas. Fractals contain a large degree of self-similarity, with increasingly miniaturized copies of themselves buried deep within the original, and infinite detail. The building's facade constantly changes. The stone laminations are translucent, glowing on the interior by day and on the exterior by night. The pattern thus continually adapts and transforms the urban facade. The three glass setbacks cause the stone volumes to suspend over the street, integrating city land-scapes into the filter zones of the facade—soft zones that suggest urban continuity.

The building typology is shifted according to urban force fields, creating the super-flat street facade and the voluptuous free space at the garden. Diagram of building transformation: the normal state plus the shifted condition results in the fragmented space (right).

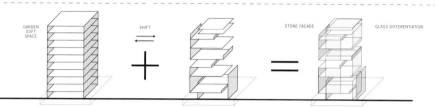

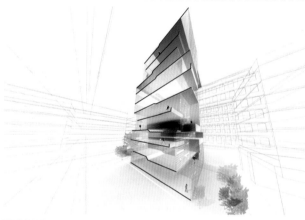

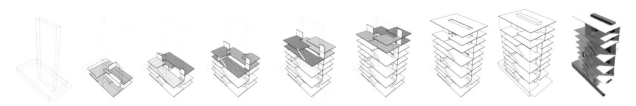

SHIFT The very different characteristics for the front and back facades of these new Tribeca lofts causes a shifted typology, where the traditional building volume is delaminated into multiple zones. The first (street) zone consists of two suspended stone volumes; the second zone is the overlap where spatial shifts happen; and the third (green) zone has three transparent volumes of glass that cantilever freely over the garden.

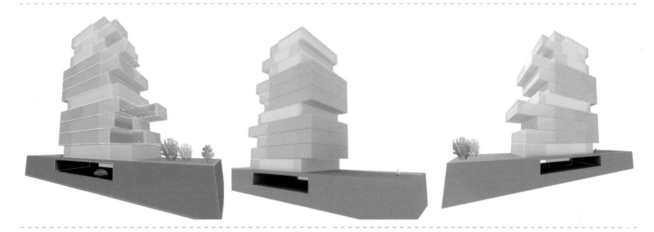

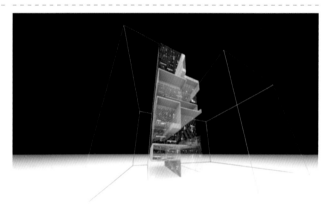

A custom-designed curtain wall
of stone and glass ranging from
opaque to translucent adds a
modern touch to this otherwise
traditional landmark neighborhood.

The definition of a random pattern notes more than just the surface; it defines the essence of the structure: **RAN·DOM** *adj* **1.** done, chosen, or occurring without a specific pattern, plan, or connection; **2.** with a pattern or in sizes that are not uniform or regular; **3.** relating or belonging to a set in which all the members have the same probability of occurrence; **4.** relating to or involving variables that have undetermined value but definite probability

—*Encarta World English Dictionary*, s.v. "Random."

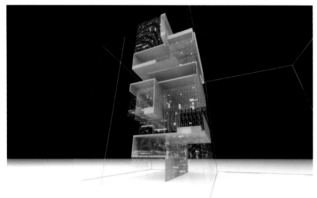

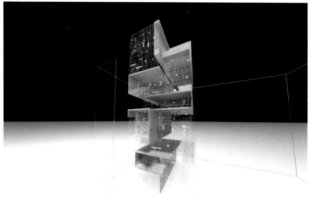

MIAMI DATA Total housing units: 148,554; 100 %//1-unit, detached: 45,523; 30.6%//1-unit, attached: 17,049; 11.5%//2 units: 8,846; 6%//3 or 4 units: 9,623; 6.5%//5 to 9 units: 13,865; 9.3%//10 to 19 units: 12,418; 8.4%//20 or more units: 39,636; 26.7%//mobile home: 1,462; 1.0%//boat, RV, van, etc.: 132; 0.1%

Statistics and demographics: population: 362,470; 100%//sex and age: male: 180,194; 49.71%; female: 182,276; 50.29%; median age (years): 37.7 —compiled from Census 2000, Population and Housing, Miami-Dade County; and U.S. Census 2000

Type	Mixed use/residential tower
Location	Miami
Area	49,946 sq. ft.
Year	2003

Synthetic Cultural Base

A new development on the edge of the now hip and upcoming Design District of Miami incorporates a fifteen-story residential tower and a **CULTURAL BASE** with a gallery, spa, gourmet deli, and parking garage. Miami, the glamour city of the 1930s, termed the "Magic City," is just over a one hundred years old and consists of an eclectic combination of art deco, beach architecture, fashionistas, and surfer culture. The district, a unique eighteen-square block with a fast-growing design community, is located just north of downtown Miami. It features showrooms, art galleries, and design companies, and it has become a city hotspot. Designed by new-urbanist Andreas Duany and inspired by developer Craig Robbins, the pedestrian-oriented area has flourished since its start in 1994 and has become a desirable place to visit and live.

Biscayne Boulevard, the site for this new development and tower, was originally an urban boulevard lined with 1940s motels that dilapidated into a derelict area with prostitution and drugs. Indicative of the city, its population is extremely diverse, a **SYNTHETIC CULTURE**: a global mix, rather than a local authenticity. Revitalized, the strip has transformed into a fashionable location between the Design District and the recently completed convention center.

The proposed urban beach tower, a tropical residential high-rise, adds a new housing typology to Miami, typically made up of low-rise residential neighborhoods. Conceived as a compilation of villas in the sky, the structure features two-, three-, or four-story apartments that hover over a synthetic cultural base. This base, topped with a large, elevated garden, negotiates the hard edge of Biscayne Boulevard with an attractive commercial program and lifts the tower above the city to provide a gorgeous, uninterrupted view of the bay.

The soft form of the tower with rounded edges resembles a beach-worn pebble, created from the friction of sand and water. Recalling Edmund Husserl's theory of **THING-SHAPES**, in which an essential form becomes recognizable through a method of difference, the tower is developed as a smooth shape with a high level of variation—temporal modulations that react to hard and soft urban pressures. The adjusted, fragmented shape allows for the intersection of different programmatic volumes; apartments, terraces, and infrastructure intertwine and overlap.

The two apartments per floor offer luxurious modern living; floating mezzanines connect the floors and allow for double-height ceilings and windows with panoramic views over the water. An extreme amount of service is expected and provided; the gallery, spa, and restaurant create a hotel-like atmosphere, with comfort and individuality as well as social hubs to be used by all.

SYNTHETIC CULTURE Miami, with its typically suburban beach culture, has been redeveloped as an urban art hub, led by the new Design District. Biscayne Boulevard, the connector between this district and the convention center area, is the axis along which new developments are quickly built-up, including this large residential tower complex.

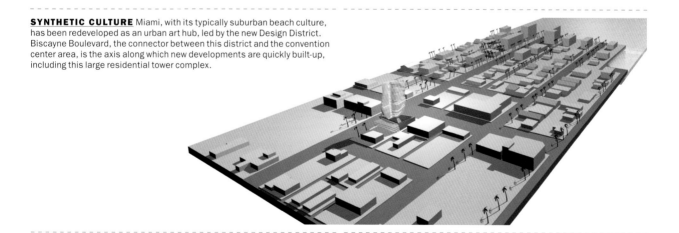

CULTURAL BASE The elevated loft tower hovers over the roof garden of the cultural base, an urban generator that contains art gallery, coffee shop, spa, and parking.

THING-SHAPES The location at a turbulent corner site results in a soft tower or thing-shape. Specific to these thing-shapes in their relationship to the human body are their "surfaces—more or less 'smooth,' more or less perfect."[1] The tower with its curved skin fluidly adapts to the differentiated multi-level loft spaces inside. Multifaceted, it allows for multiple uses and views.

[1] *Edmund Husserl's Origin of Geometry*, introduction by Jacques Derrida (Lincoln, NE: University of Nebraska, 1962).

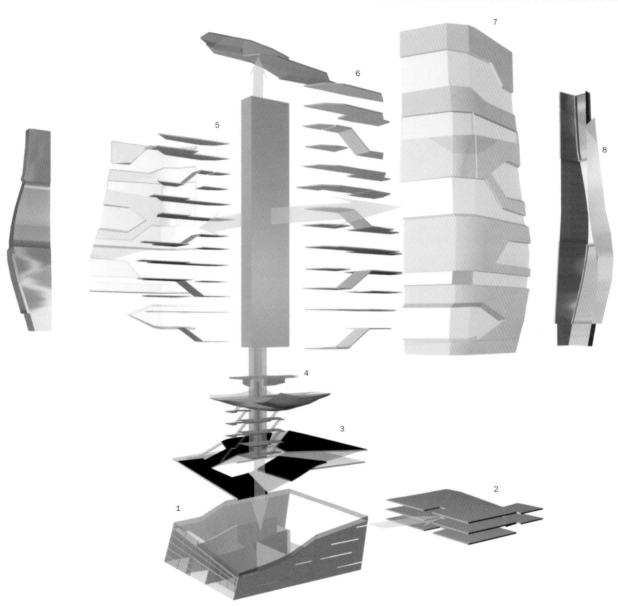

1. cultural base; 2. parking; 3. elevated garden; 4. infrastructure; 5. core; 6. mezzanine floors; 7. aluminum custom facade components; 8. glass skin

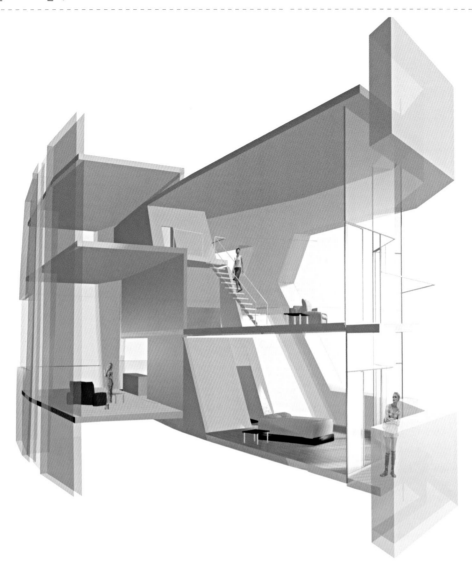

The lofts are designed to be villas in the sky. Each floor has two interlocking split-level units with generous areas, 20-foot glass facades, double-height living rooms, and large exterior spaces that make for a modern living scenario. Hotel-like services are provided to add to luxury and ease of living.

duplex plan 1F

duplex plan 2F

Type   Residential lofts
Location Utrecht, the Netherlands
Area   185,000 sq. ft.
Year   2004

The typical Dutch house has been delaminated in overlapping private and public layers (left), throwing domesticity into question and proposing a loose urban lifestyle.

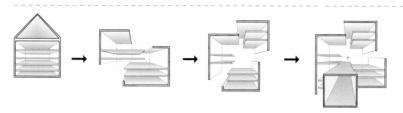

URBAN ATTRACTOR An attractor typically is a fixed point or state of equilibrium that a system behavior is drawn to and tends to imitate. Here, in Utrecht, a university town in Holland, an existing school structure will be renovated and flanked by urban loft buildings, inserting a new lifestyle at the edge of the city center—potentially causing a shift in the urban migration and population patterns.

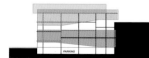

U2 Urban Lofts

Utrecht, a university town in the Netherlands, is redeveloping its city center and inserting a new lifestyle into the area. Located at the edge of the center, across from a beautiful park, sits a 1930s school building, which will be extended with modern housing units planned around a green courtyard. These generous apartments will become an **ATTRACTOR** for urban living, and, through the introduction of diverse lifestyles, the area will change from within.

The urban block as a type is delaminated; the individual units are shifted and overlapped, thus informing each other while adding a set of in-between fractured spaces. The **DELAMINATION** of the planes not only creates an interesting repositioning of the units within the larger whole, but also a thick skin to be occupied. This thickened facade, with transparencies, translucencies, and overlaps, blurs the inside and outside spaces, suspends living areas within its layers, and cantilevers volumes out and over the urban landscape. The layered skin becomes architecture—a temporal modulation mediating between city and living room.

The modulation, as a dynamic organism, allows the building to hover in an undetermined state, forever becoming. This instability provides clear individuality in the units and ambiguity in the common areas. The overlaps, which create the in-between spaces, cause fractures—small flaws in the structure. Flaws as they are found in crystals are infinitely small, but significant. The **QUASI-CRYSTAL**, with its seemingly spontaneous organization, forms another sense of order—an aperiodic structure called the "Penrose tiles." It is not the crystalline structure that is of interest here, as its structural unit is repeated in space in a strictly periodic way, but the quasi-crystal: the most organized of all, in its predictable unpredictability.

The new apartments adjacent to the school in their shifted interiority destabilize and activate the static condition of the eighteenth-century city. These shifts allow for a productive tension between public access and interior privacy, providing oblique views—glimpses of urban fragments reflected in the shimmering glass surfaces. Three housing types are suspended in the super blocks: the open loft, urban villa, and split-level apartment. As they are equipped with modern systems and comfort, each has its own intricate spatial configuration, creating differentiation through the repetition of the units. Their crystal-like structure mediates nature and order. The super blocks integrate layers of green zones for relaxation and play, a filter space to the surrounding city.

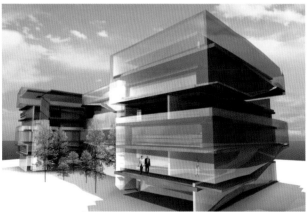

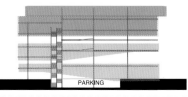

Variation I: open courtyard: entrance level

typical upper level

DELAMINATION Living within the delaminated transparent and translucent surfaces of the facade creates loose living environments with a high
level of flexibility. Several split-level apartments are inserted and negotiate
through multi-story hallways. These public zones connect through fractures,
allowing for domestic continuity and a smooth connection to the city.

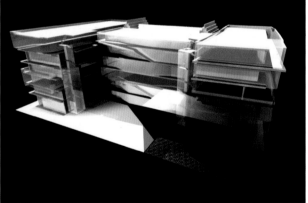

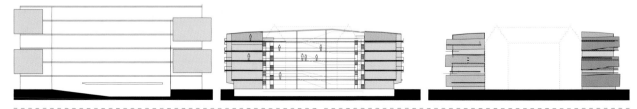

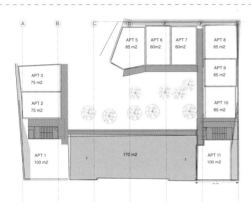

Variation II: closed courtyard: entrance level

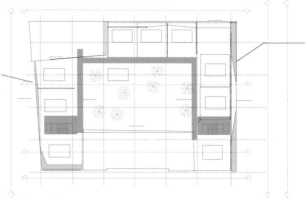

typical upper level

QUASI-CRYSTAL In 1972 the English mathematician R. Penrose developed a special apparatus to describe aperiodic structures, termed the "Penrose tiles." Covering planar space with two simple polygons called the "golden" regular rhombs, Penrose unveiled the quasi-crystal. A high level of multiplicity differentiates the quasi-crystal from conventional metallic alloys. A new order in a seemingly disorderly organization, the crystalline structure proposes a lattice of shifted housing units, where through misalignment new infrastructural spaces occur.

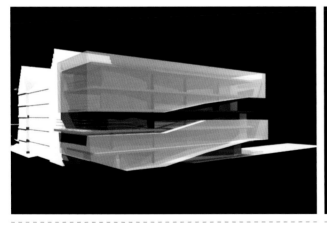

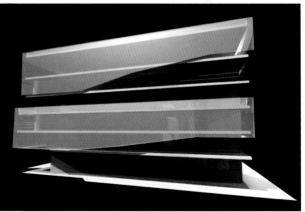

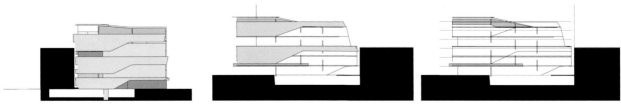

The intelligence of industrial design is best exemplified in the layering of the integral motorbike helmet. Here, each layer is an essential part of the whole assembly. The hard shiny shell protects against shock impact and the more interesting layer of integral foam negotiates the perfect spherical shape of the helmet with the imperfect shape of the head, and provides ventilation and sound systems. The multi-tasking foam layer inspired the development of the Aida smart-wall system.

Aida Salon

Type Salon
Location New York City
Area 2,000 sq. ft.
Year 2000

The **CREASE** as a hybrid construct is investigated as a set of "smart," adaptable, smooth walls in the Aida Salon, located on the Upper East Side of Manhattan. Aida's owner desired an innovative contemporary hair salon that would redefine the outdated styles of her two existing salons and introduce a new program to attract and invite an expanded clientele—young and fashionable—into the 2,000-square-foot space. The salon's program explicitly includes hair cutting and washing stations, manicure and pedicure areas, and a massage and dressing room. Maintenance and durability are of great importance, as is modern comfort.

A reconceptualization and deconstruction of the traditional hair salon is examined through an analysis of the salon's program, generating a **SMOOTH WRAPPER**—a smart wall system that integrates progressive lighting; heating, cooling, and sound systems; and storage. A precise spatial modulation results; deflection and inflection of the wall's continuous surfaces redefine the remaining area into a sculpted void generating a new type of space for a new type of clientele.

The wrapper negotiates both the urban landscape (hard space) as well the private domain (soft space). Disseminating the soft in the hard and the hard in the soft, the smart wall encapsulates the human body while demanding minimum space and providing maximum comfort and efficiency. As in the design of the integral motorbike helmet, the salon's walls are layered and delaminated. The helmet has an outer layer, a hard shiny shell, which protects against weather (rain, wind) and forces (traffic accidents, impact). The second layer, the most intelligent layer, negotiates between two systems: the shell's perfect sphere and the imperfect form of the human head. This integrated foam layer creates an amorphous shape configured by negotiating the imprint of its two adjacencies, the body and the shell. It adds softness and impact protection and allows for incorporated amenities like sound speakers and ventilation systems. It is an informed, intelligent layer, constantly providing and adjusting to achieve ultimate economy and comfort. This performance-driven behavior informs the smart walls of the salon; the mark of efficiency of use, the registration of areas of ease allows for an organic formulation of space, thus negotiating desire with facility.

Inside, this wrapper reorganizes all of the programmatic requirements for an efficient work environment, all evenly distributed. Creases allow for local insertions of cutting stations, lighting, and seating elements. Essential for the **SYSTEM**, the smart skin operates not as an object, but as an integral part of a structure of informed smooth surfaces, generating and regenerating the space. The salon creates and enacts its own drama; within the sculpted space, integrated light sources and mirror surfaces play with vision lines and angles, reflecting and superimposing images and spatial folds.

At the exterior, two interfaces further define this health-style program: a bamboo garden creates a relaxed waiting area at the back and a folded stone-and-glass facade mediates between city and salon. This asymmetric facade is a continuation of the interior wrapper; it hardens to protect and creases to soften and dissolve the exterior boundary. This succeeds in drawing clients in, initiating a sense of truly contemporary space and emphasizing the sense of comfort throughout.

SMOOTH WRAPPER Aida was the first project that dealt with the idea of a "smart" architecture, which operates like a smart car. Integrating the operations of the salon into a wrapper or wall system allowed for an analysis of performative operational tasks, essential to the smart surfaces as they modulate the remaining space.

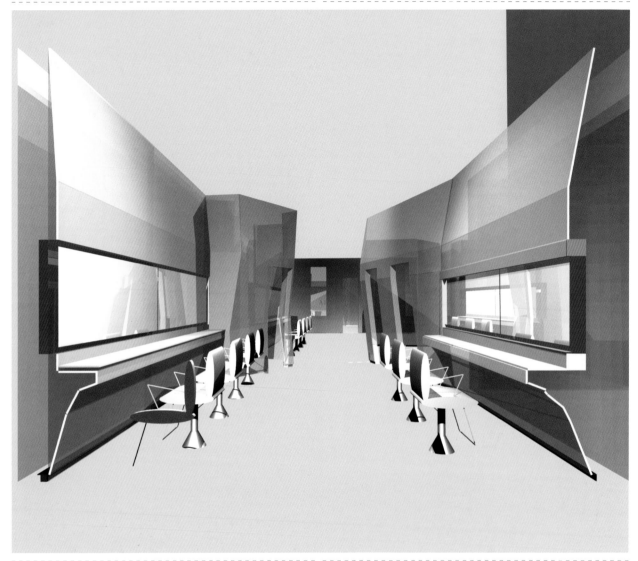

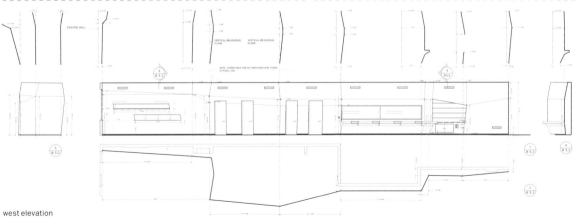

west elevation

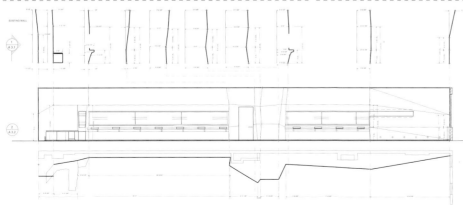

Detailed elevations and sections indicating x, y, and z work points for spatial folds

east elevation

SYSTEM-BASED A system is "a combination of related elements organized into a complex whole through a methodical set of procedures; it is
composed of a set of organs or structures in the body that have a common
function."[1] Here, this is exemplified in architecture as an assembly of
mechanical or electronic components that function together as a unit. The
"smart wall" integrates systems of lighting, air conditioning, and sound and
encapsulates floating mirrors, workstations, and massage and dressing
rooms in its folded/creased surfaces.

[1] *Encarta World English Dictionary*, s.v. "System."

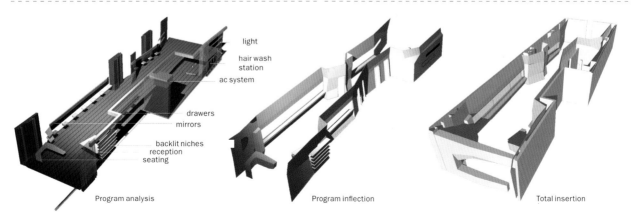

light

hair wash station

ac system

drawers

mirrors

backlit niches
reception
seating

Program analysis

Program inflection

Total insertion

OBLIQUE The facade, with its slanting and sloping geometry, hovers in an oblique state. The organic character of the long stretched lines crossing the facade recalls anatomy—a system of oblique muscles or ligaments that run along the structure's face. In fact, the cultural institution as a political instrument instigates oblique public commentaries to direct situations in its art exhibits and publications.

ArtSpace

Type   Gallery; invited
            competition
Location   New York City
Area   13,655 sq. ft.
Year   2004

A new high-rise development in Midtown Manhattan features a *kunsthal*, a modern art gallery, contained in the complex's base with an adjacent lobby and parking garage above. An outdoor courtyard provides a sculpture garden, art cafe, and cantilevered lounge for the gallery.

The incredible scale of this large urban project creates a great opportunity to express the impact of this emerging cultural hub for the city. By integrating the facade of the parking garage into the gallery facade, the curtain wall of the base is transformed, its surface slowly segmenting and morphing into an independent entity—a **METAMERE**. The metameric facade transitions away from a normative curtain wall into a transformative, programmatically encoded surface. A new organic system is formed for the art unit, which, as part of a larger whole, becomes a node in the international art scene. This metamorphosis allows the *kunsthal* its own identity, a complete and marked change in its physical form, structure, and substance.

The distortion of the facade continues inside with the spiraling and unfolding of the floor plates and wall surfaces, creating a set of **EVOLUTIONS** in space. The goal of the metamere is to maintain utmost continuity and total spatial flexibility; floor segments form a natural division of space that adapts through sliding and folding mechanisms. Approximately four different gallery arrangements (from one to five zones) are feasible, but other multiple variations may be considered.

The slowly ramping topology extends throughout the different art zones and leads to the enclosed garden and cafe. Through the **OBLIQUE** cuts and surface folds of the facade, the visitor encounters glimpses of the exhibition spaces and the city, as well as the sculpture garden. The urban facade topology, the metamere, separates into opaque and transparent surfaces to allow traces of light to filter in, and the interior topology allows spatial event gaps to occur. Time and space are registered on its surfaces.

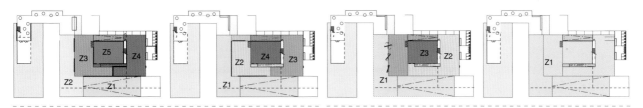

Density variations from maximum to minimum (above left to right). Facade transformation (below left to right): recode gallery facade, deregulate mullions, generate facade topography, potential facade variation

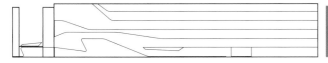

EVOLUTION Spatial continuity through temporality is introduced as a set of spiraling planar devices. The spiral, as a curved plane circling about its center, is in an extreme form—a continuous series of loops, a whorl of spaces. The unwinding spatial configurations of floor and wall surfaces allow for overview and separation, openness and privacy. The exhibition reveals itself slowly to the passerby and unfolds in an endless array of galleries.

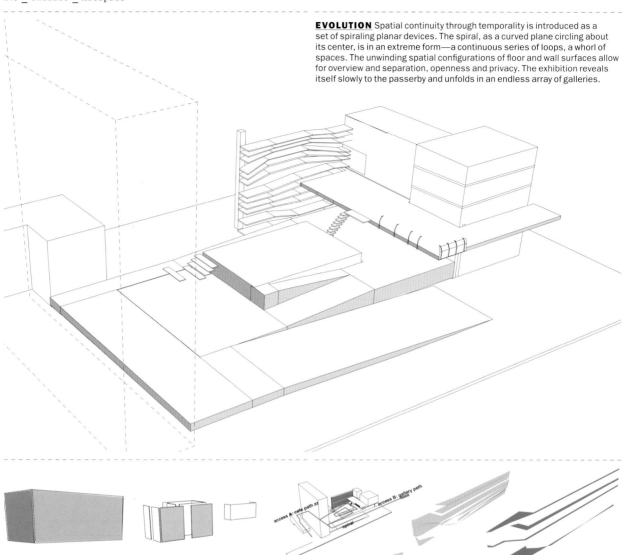

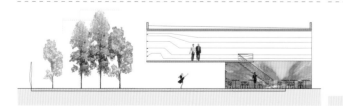

Diagram showing (above left to right): 13,655 sq. ft. box reinterpreted; adjustable gallery walls; two systems: spiral loop flow and cross flow; envelope: opaque strips; envelope: transparent strips

The ArtSpace activates a small public garden; the cafe is cantilevered over the garden exhibit and allows for glimpses of the city.

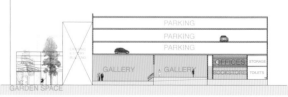

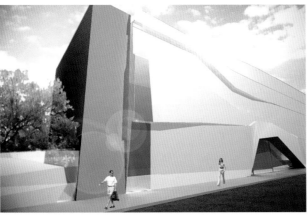

METAMERE The condition of a metamere that divides a body into a series of similar (not the same) segments exemplifies the facade's variation of the grid's repetition. The crisis of the grid, now animated—distorted and adapted into another state—signifies the specific urban condition of the ArtSpace within the larger complex.

SMART ROOM A modular system that performs a multiplicity of functions, the smart room acts as a pivotal point around which areas reorganize; it is the digital main frame of the gallery and it creates the "branding" of the Bitforms digital gallery concept worldwide.

Type	Digital gallery
Location	New York City
Area	1,600 sq. ft.
Year	2001

A set of frameless translucent Plexiglas daylight projection screens communicates between gallery, smart room, and office. Every surface here is a digital communication device.

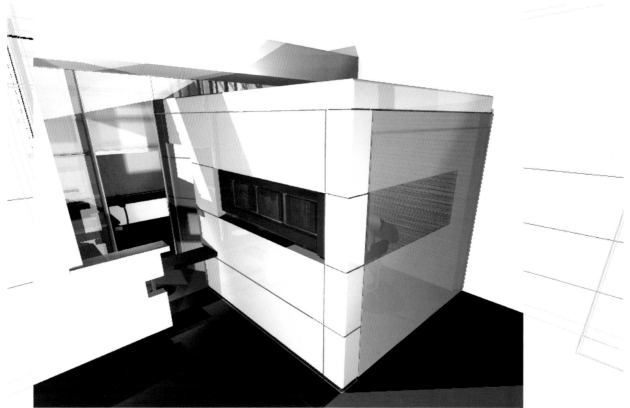

Bitforms

Bitforms is a new digital gallery located in New York City's Chelsea district, known for its emerging collection of exhibition spaces. A particularly cutting-edge gallery, Bitforms exhibits work based only on electronic and digital means, creating a synthesis of art and technology.

The design for the gallery space expands on digital and virtual concepts and encompasses the most specific, minimal, and effective move—a multifunctional "**SMART ROOM**." The room marks the critical point where several programs, such as a meeting area, reception, and gallery, spatially overlap. Functioning as a private presentation space and conference room, it also contains the mainframe and memory of the gallery—two flat touch screens suspended in a pivoting steel structure. This adaptable **INTERFACE** can be integrated into the exhibit, provide for individual or closed screenings within the room, or act as a digital archival unit for the gallery's recent and current exhibitions. As event space, the pivotal wall segment activates the gallery and is interactive to its users.

The modular smart room is constructed with industrial-design precision; an aluminum frame clad with bent aluminum panels, pivoting doors, and acoustic wall units results in a **PREFAB** structure with soft corners. One side of the room features a large white translucent screen, which creates visual contact with the gallery (silhouettes of visitors), or acts as a projection surface. The room is completely set up for electronic communication and digital presentations that extend throughout the gallery in a sequence of pre-wired plug-in bands, allowing for digital artwork to be displayed with invisible connections, and contains built-in lighting and music systems, all to produce an interactive art environment.

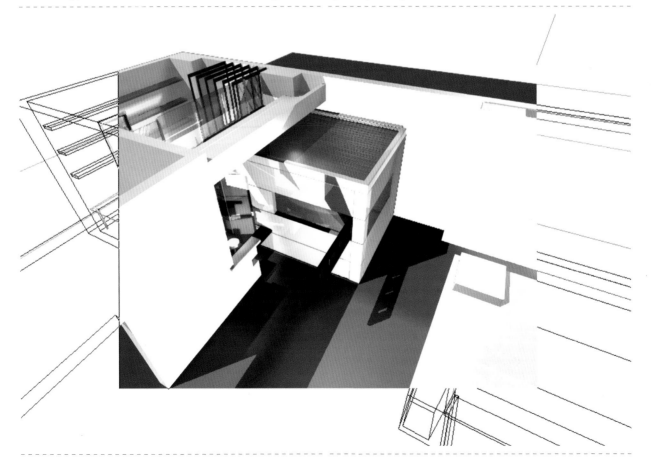

PREFAB MODULE The smart room is manufactured of a light aluminum frame with custom bent aluminum panels. All data wiring, heating, cooling, and lighting are contained in one simple prefab system.

DIGITAL INTERFACE A pivoting unit is inserted in the smart room; an integral steel frame holds two flat touch screens suspending data that informs the visitor of past, present, and upcoming art installations and exhibits. The unit can thus be part of the exhibit, a flat data information wall unit, or a digital presentation screen for clients in the private meeting room.

TOPOLOGICAL BANDS Mathematical deformations, which operate over time in a relational manner, are coded with specific programmatic data; the topological bands, and thus the programs, intersect and overlap urban life and museum events in an open-weave structure.

Type   Museum; competition
Location Goteborg, Sweden
Area   120,000 sq. ft.
Year   1998

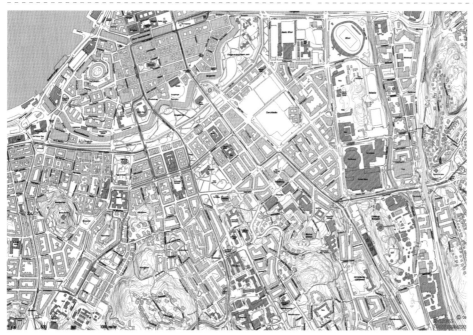

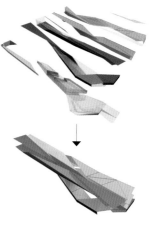

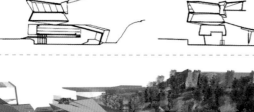

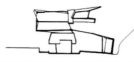

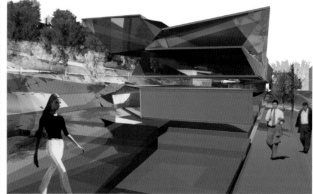

Museum of World Culture

Virtual textures, as discussed here, relate to the constant flow of communication and new media. The modern museum has transgressed the institution as a singular unit to become a node in the **NETWORK** of universities, libraries, and other museums. The real-time space of communication, which connects each of us to a global matrix, can no longer be visualized. The new computer network spaces, such as the World Wide Web, bring more information on a broader level. These communication systems change the importance of the location or site of the built structure. Buildings can be located anywhere—in the middle of the desert, or underground in the city—less a physical representation of power than a node in the global network of information systems.

In his 1955 essay "The Question Concerning Technology," Martin Heidegger describes the culture of man as a development that expresses itself both in art and science. Art is defined as the spiritual manifestation of this culture and science as the "theory of the real." Theory is understood as observation (*betrachtung*) of the real as "that which works," or as the verb "to do," which goes back to the Greek term "thesis"—the setting, place, position. Thus architecture can be described as a cultural expression that observes that which works—a network, a place. With its electronic library, digital archive, and interactive exhibits, this museum will become one of these nodes in the ongoing discussion on the relevance of art and architecture.

Situated in a steep hillside flanking an institution-lined avenue, the museum creates the beginnings of a cultural hub in Goteborg. The interest lies in the investigation of the deformation of topological surfaces as a continuous programmatic device. Unlike Le Corbusier's elevated *piloti* structure of the 1930s, the museum is developed from interweaving bands unfolding from the landscape, as an integrated part of the urban geography. The weaving and twisting bands are performance driven, a dynamic **SYSTEM** that connects and informs, represented in a three-dimensional programmatic matrix that replaces the two-dimensional Euclidian grid. Two topological surfaces are generated; the first, the urban ribbon, intersects and links with the second, the exhibition surface. At this intersection, the museum transforms from a public urban space with a digital library, cyber-cafe, and print workshops into an interactive exhibition space with a high level of surveillance. Both surfaces are fluidly connected as well as separated and create various overlapping environments.

Spaces consisting of a series of dynamic frames, modulations, and shifting horizons alter the common notions of

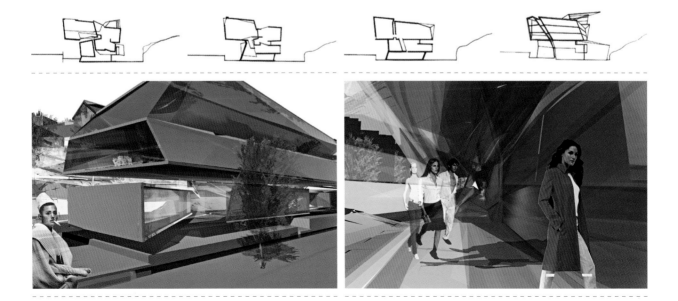

architectural elements such as the wall, ceiling, and floor. These traditional boundaries become **TOPOLOGICAL BANDS**, forming connective membranes and electronic devices. The alternating transparent and opaque surfaces continue in the horizontal as well as the vertical planes and provide indirect light that reflects off the wall and floor planes to create a spectacular play of daylight and views, constantly transforming the spatial experience of the museum. The introduction of reinforced composite surface materials prevents the use of heavy load-bearing elements and enhances the fluid reading of the building, allowing for innovative maintenance-free solutions, while adding to the durability of the structural skin. This typology proposes a building as landscape, with an integral datascape informing its immediate and remote environments.

NETWORK The museum as a node in a network of education, culture, and electronic media establishes the city of Goteborg in the large global information system.

1. storage; 2. darkrooms; 3. entry; 4. cyber cafe; 5. library; 6. ramp to exhibition; 7. exhibition space; 8. private galleries; 9. upper gallery; 10. upper exhibition; 11. offices

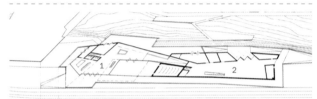

basement

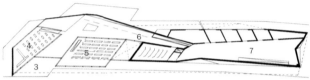

entry level

INTEGRAL SYSTEM The museum is not developed as the generic Domino structure with columns and floor plates, but as a set of structural bands that fold out of the site's topography to form a connective tissue of exhibition spaces. Transparent and opaque surfaces unwind from floor to wall to ceiling; a play of light and dark folds reveals the exhibit at unexpected, intriguing angles.

second floor

third floor

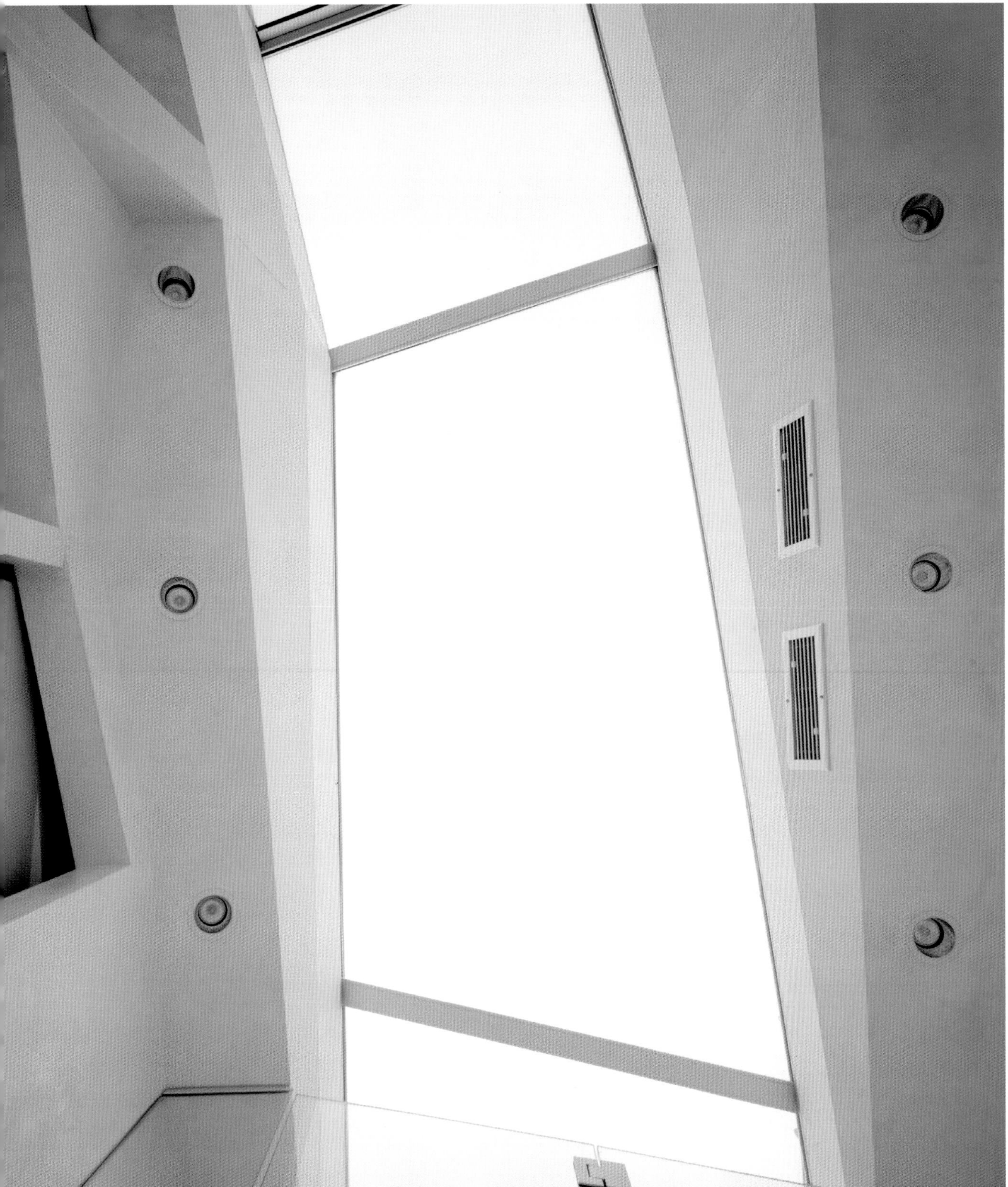

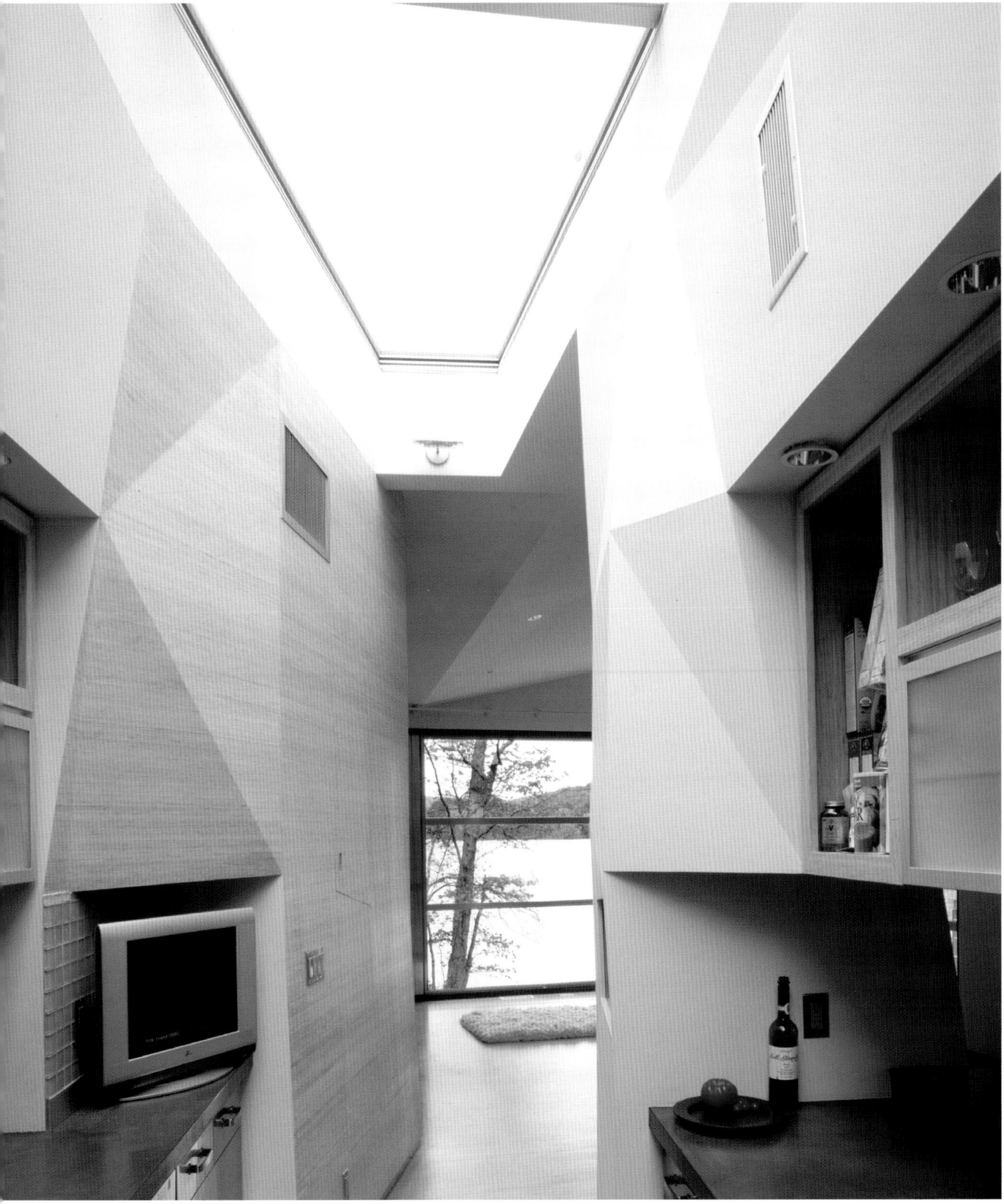

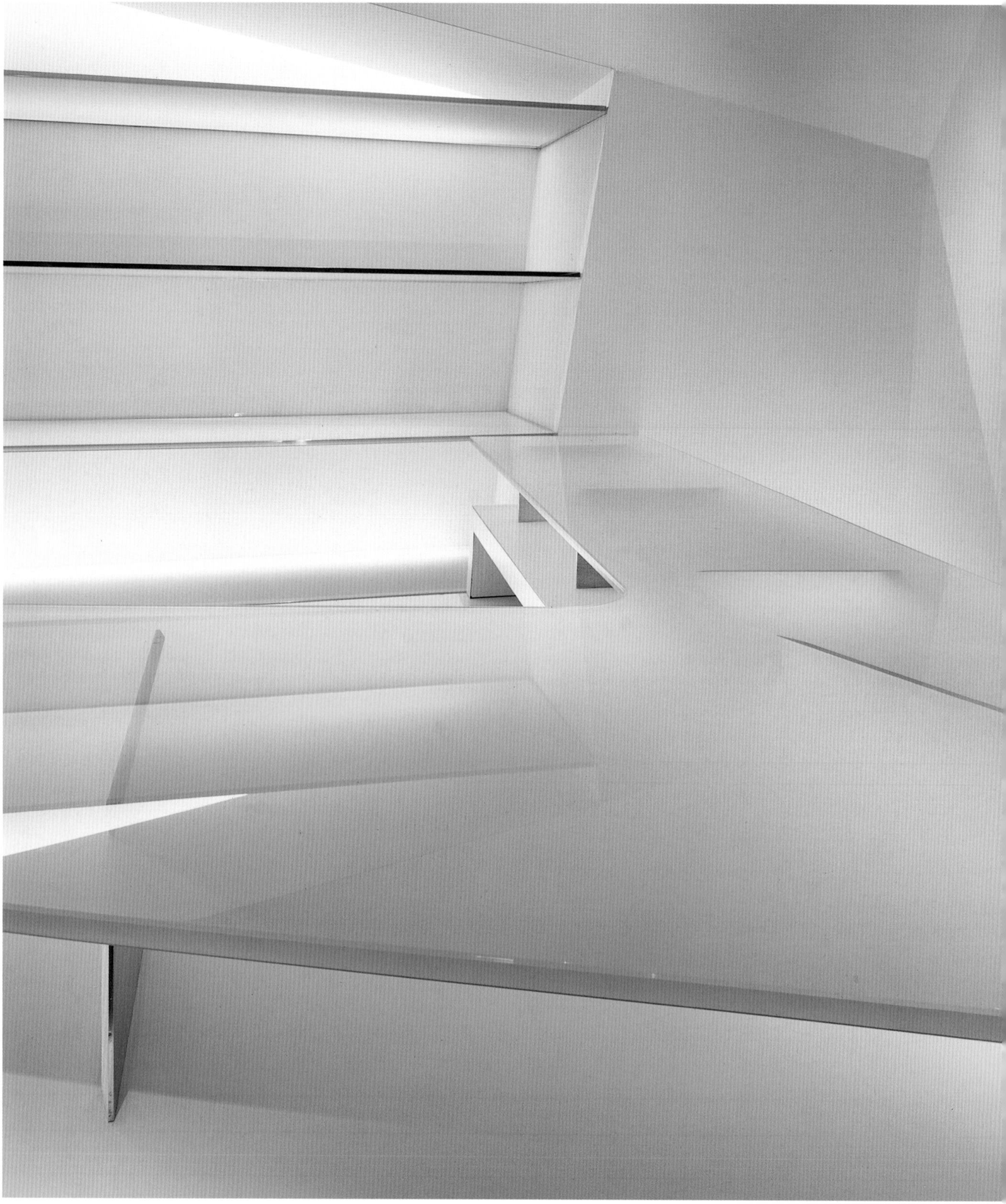

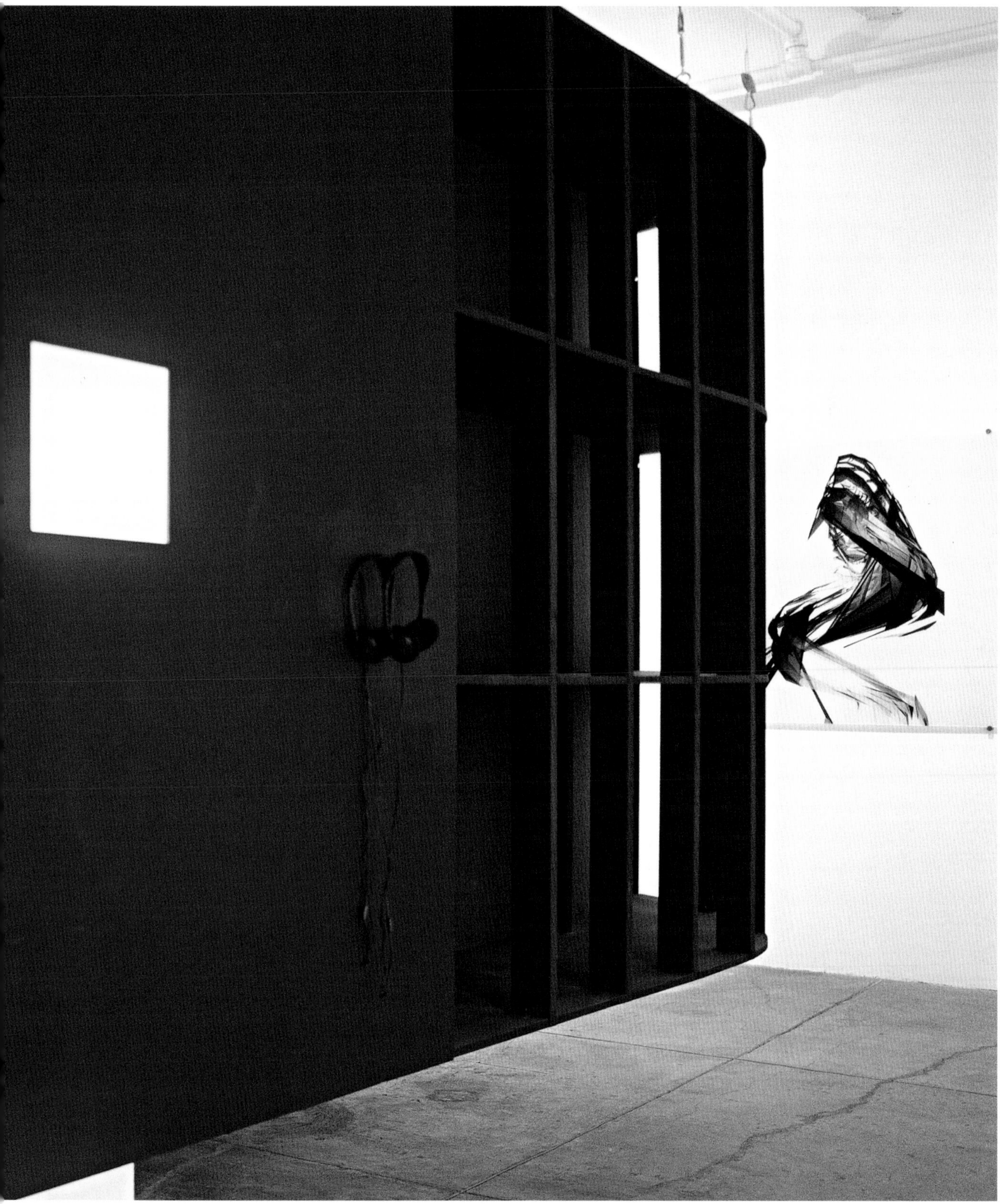

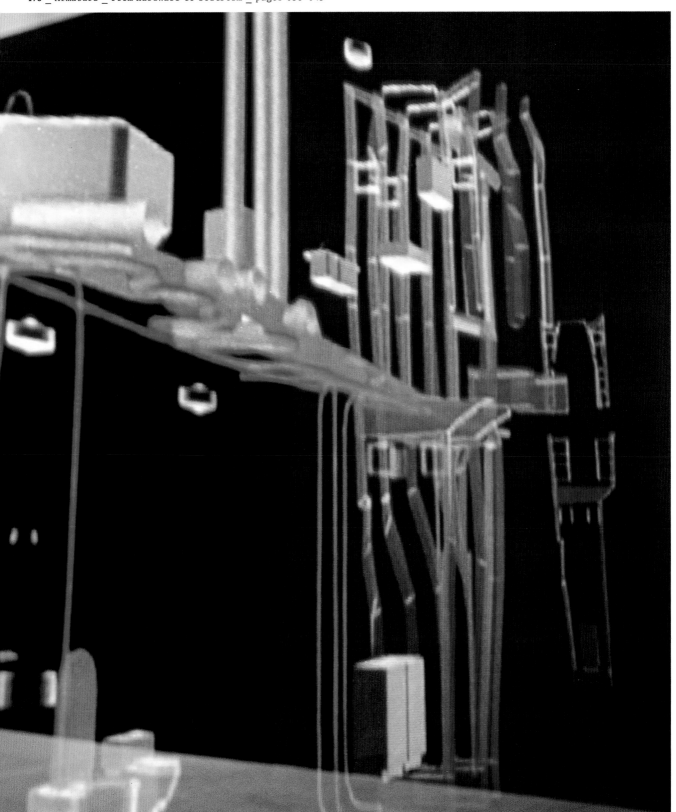

IN·TER·FACE *n* **1.** the surface, place, or point where two things touch each other or meet **2.** a common boundary between objects or different phases of a substance **3.** the place, situation, or way in which two things or people act together or affect each other or the point of connection between things **4.** a common boundary shared by two devices, or by a person and a device, across which data or information flows, for example, the screen of a computer **5.** software that links a computer with another device, or the set of commands, messages, images, and other allowing communication between computer and operator **6.** an electronic device or circuit or other point of contact between two pieces of equipment; *vt* **1.** to touch or meet at a surface, place, or point, or to make things join in this way **2.** to act together or affect each other or to make things or people interact **3.** to connect or serve as an interface for two or more pieces of equipment

—*Encarta World English Dictionary*, s.v. "Interface."

inter face

URBAN FABRICS co-evolve through simultaneous operation as dynamic urban catalysts and interactive digital environments. Urban dynamics are investigated through two media: the dynamic frame and the interactive interface. Framing is essentially a filmic device, creating a geometric and physical boundary that contains meaning, effect, and emotion. The rearview mirror not only provides a glance of the past, but also of our memory of that past; it combines effect and affect. "Framing is limitation," Gilles Deleuze states, "but depending on the concept itself the limits can be conceived in two ways, mathematically or dynamically."[1] The dynamics studied utilize mathematics as a method of probability, extrapolating information from the past to a possible future—the event-horizon.

The interface on the other hand is neutral. Situated between the virtual and the viewer, it negotiates communication flows. As in animation (electronic transmission), the interface's analogue is found in a virtual system and its elements in data. But where in animation form is created by time, the interface performs over time. As an interactive device, its encrypted code translates data from the virtual world to the real—sets of higher-dimensional worlds collide, connect, and overlap and boundaries dissolve.

The time-images of the collapse of the World Trade Center represent altered urban data fields. These images show a view of downtown Manhattan on September 10, 2001 and an altered view on September 14, 2001.

[1] Gilles Deleuze, *Cinema 1: Movement-Image* (London: Athlone Press, 1986), 13.

Urban Field

Design Intelligence: Winka Dubbeldam
Michael Speaks

Speaks: There is a signature approach that many now associate with Dutch design driven by the pragmatic analysis and use of data and information. And there is also a signature design associated with the theoretical and digital work that emerged at about the same time from Columbia University, in New York. Your work seems a combination of both? **Dubbeldam:** Yes, I suppose that might be true. I studied for my first degree in the Netherlands. But there was little theory or interest in theory in the schools there. I worked with Joost Meuwissen and Wim Nijenhuis who were both interested in Gilles Deleuze and Paul Virilio, but there was not much else happening in philosophy or theory otherwise. I was always interested in Deleuze because his approach was generative rather than reflective. My interest was not literal in the way many architects later adapted Deleuze to form making; on the contrary, I was interested in an approach or process that was generative and inspired by Deleuze. When I read his work it seemed so spatial to me. I was especially interested in the behavior of systems and morphogenesis and Deleuze informed my thinking about both. None of these issues was surfacing in the Netherlands, no one was reading or working with them. After I graduated, I felt it was too early to open my own office, and, to be honest, I had worked for almost all of the people I was interested in. Also, I wanted to focus on a more theoretical approach. After considering the AA in London, I decided to go to Columbia University for a post-graduate degree. **Speaks:** What was Columbia like in the early 1990s? **Dubbeldam:** It was an amazing time to be there. Immediately I became very interested in the debates about weak and strong form that Jeffrey Kipnis and Peter Eisenman were then discussing. Reviews included people like Kipnis, Michael Hays, Mark Taylor, and strong young voices like Hani Rashid and Stan Allen, who were teaching there. Columbia enabled me to read and work through theory for a year, to deal with these issues in a place where there was an active debate. I was really interested to find out what, if anything, theory could contribute to architecture. To be honest, I was not sure at that point if theory could be implemented in architectural practice. Eisenman was on my final review at Columbia and I was impressed with his confidence in the relationship between architecture and theory. It convinced me that theory had a role to play. I went to work for him not too long after that. **Speaks:** What software were people working with then? **Dubbeldam:** When I came to New York in 1990 hardly anyone had computers in their offices. No one was working or designing digitally. I had worked for Steven Holl and Bernard Tschumi in 1990 and 1991 before enrolling in the AAD Program at Columbia. There were hardly any computers in those offices nor were there any in the studios at the school. There was only one computer lab. I was one of the few in the program working digitally. Most were drawing by hand. I worked with some Japanese friends, kind of computer nerds, and we worked in their studio, not at Columbia. **Speaks:** So when did you start working digitally? **Dubbeldam:** My thesis in Holland in 1990 was generated on the computer. I was a computer freak: very interested in animation and three-dimensional software. Eisenman's was the first office I worked for that was comfortably digital. We mostly used form-Z. I was there two years and among other things worked on an urban plan for Dusseldorf. It was very exciting; I collaborated with a physicist friend of mine and was able to play out some of the ideas I had studied at Columbia. The site was challenging because it was not a plane but a virtual three-dimensional volume blanketed by a roof of radar and radio waves that could not be penetrated due to interference with airplanes landing nearby. We knew all the points of the towers and we calculated the exact frequencies of all the waves and created an interference field over the site. This was translated into a topological field of information that was projected as a generative force. The inflection of the data field and the physical site started to designate areas of occupation. These reflected the "flow" of information and created a dynamic urban scheme. **Speaks:** That seems like such an Eisenman way of generating form. But your own work seems to depart from that? **Dubbeldam:** Yes, that is true. Peter stops the research before other layers of information—social, political, economic—are added. I learned a great deal working there but ultimately I wanted to expand the research beyond form generation. **Speaks:** You left Eisenman's after two years and opened your own office, Archi-Tectonics? **Dubbeldam:** Yes, I opened an office and started to teach theory at Parsons and a design studio at Columbia. Suddenly a lot of things began to happen, including an exhibition of my work at Form Zero gallery in Los Angeles. It was mostly work I had done since leaving the Netherlands and included several competitions. Looking back on it now, this work—which was published as a monograph—was really an exploratory period that enabled me to pursue the kind of intellectual and formal issues that brought me to New York to begin with. **Speaks:** And you were faced with real projects. **Dubbeldam:** Yes, the first one was the Cristine Rose Gallery in SoHo in New York. The gallery had recently been sold to my client; the interior was done for the previous owner by Richard Gluckman and was perfect. But there was no special facade or clear entry area. The project became a three-foot-deep "electronic" skin that wrapped the front facade, transformed into a courtyard wall, and ultimately created the entrance to the gallery and courtyard. I wanted to make an interactive information wall. Where you might normally find windows, I placed four monitors, each of which was connected to a camera focused on a different room in the gallery. It was an inverted surveillance system but on occasion the monitors also showed the work of video artists. The project was a lot about the inversion of the role of art in the public and private realms, and about bringing art onto the street using surveillance technology. **Speaks:** And what is the diagram etched on the facade? **Dubbeldam:** I etched the zero-age main sequence diagram into the glass windows of the existing facade that shows the lifespan of a star—it is born, lives, and implodes in a black hole. It was a comment on the five-year life span of an artist in New York, and ironically the gallery remained there five years before it moved to Chelsea. The temporal aspect of the project was really important because what I built was not so much about the physicality of architecture but about electronic viewing and the devices. It was an electronic information set. **Speaks:** Have you ever been identified with the blob architects? Your pedigree is very similar to many of those architects? **Dubbeldam:** I was never into blob architecture. It is no different than the box. The difference in the box and the blob for me is interesting only if one is more performative than the other, if one is able to do things that the other cannot. That's what's great about the generative software we all now use: it has very specific parameters that can be programmed to test and simulate specific conditions so that we are better able to understand their behaviors. A lot of architects in the mid-1990s became fascinated with the software. By the time Maya and other animation software became a phenomena (and pushed the blob forms) I had already been working with software for some time and for me it was only a tool that enabled me to investigate things I could not otherwise. **Speaks:** And yet the connection between those softwares and the emergence of blobby forms is undeniable! **Dubbeldam:** Some architects used the software to translate information into form—it was a quite literal translation. That was not interesting to me, that kind of research. Instead, I was interested in the behavioral or performative aspects of systems—political, economic, etc.—or the performance of products and materials that could be tested and used in a real way. The formal aspect is a result of that, but it is only one among many complex data sets architects have to work with. To be an architect you need to know more than form or shape; you need to know the state of things. That is why I was more interested in the abstraction of mathematics than in the absolute values described in geometry. Geometry is of course part of mathematics, but mathematics is more abstract, it is about the state of things. When you add up the sides of a triangle they are 180 degrees; but in mathematics if you project the triangle on a convex curved surface it is more than 180 degrees and if you project it on a concave surface it is less. In mathematics you always want to know the state of the thing—is it flat, curved, whatever—then you can define it. In geometry the thing is always assumed to be flat. **Speaks:** Flex-City, your proposal for the WTC that was part of the exhibition curated by Max Protetch, seems a good example of the performativity of form and design? **Dubbeldam:** Max asked fifty architects from around the world to make a sketch about what should happen on the WTC site and these were to be exhibited in his gallery in January 2002. I had so many thoughts about this that ultimately I could not make just a sketch. I was interested in rethinking the future of Manhattan rather than jumping straight into the rebuilding of the towers. The idea was to create an interactive and investigative interface that would become a ubiquitous think-model revealing different scenarios for downtown. That, I thought, would be more fitting than new towers. It was a very Dutch approach (Rotterdam was, as you know, flattened in the war), one that comes from trying to see what new possibilities can emerge from tragedy. For those living in New York it was clear that downtown had been changing for some time before September 11. And for that reason we conducted an intense study of the economic conditions that had been driving that change. Of course September 11 did make us think differently about the tower or tall building as a symbol or expression of corporate power. I wanted to explore new typologies that would give the city a chance to become something modern and new. I was very interested in combining and differentiating horizontal office spaces and vertical housing typologies to create a hybrid city model. **Speaks:** So how does Flex-City work? **Dubbeldam:** It is an interactive electronic environment that takes into consideration four factors including the stock market, migration patterns, local politics, and tourism. We designed several new housing and office typologies that would be deployed and change over time depending on how each of the parameters was chosen by the visitors of the exhibit. The assumption was that any prediction of what might happen on the site would be based on data and on the psychological impact of data—data, in that sense, is exogenous. The electronic model allows you to visualize what happens when these parameters become interactive with the others. It is a kind of wind tunneling for the typologies that gives you some indication of how they might develop under different scenarios. **Speaks:** That raises an important issue about the relationship between research and theoretical ideas and real projects? I am thinking especially of the Greenwich Street project in Lower Manhattan, one of your first big projects to be completed? **Dubbeldam:** People talk about the folding front facade as an aesthetic thing. And of course one cannot deny that it is, but my real interest was politically and theoretically motivated. Political because I wanted to blur streetscape and private space to try and make clear that public space is in the middle of our living room—it comes through the Internet. The facade of the building is like a raincoat, just a climatological device; it provides no security—that comes instead from security systems. The electronic world has transformed the role of the facade permanently. Theoretical because the way I wanted to accomplish this was through inflection, transforming the two-dimensional plane into a three-dimensional world, something Bernard Cache talks a lot about in his book *Earth Moves*. Inflecting the planes create new spaces, transitions, and ambiguities. But it also deals with pragmatic issues like setback rules. For example, employing inflection allows the skin to become a single performative system rather than a device that separates. The folds in the facade are diagonal which means the whole space folds inside out and is pulled unlike if it were a simple fold. But this can only be controlled with the kind of precision three-dimensional computer modeling makes possible. During the design phase the slightest change in the fold—whether for code or aesthetic reasons—affected the entire building because it was all one performative system. This also meant that with fabrication everything was controlled by mathematics, by an abstract system rather than by traditional site measurements. This leads to a completely different way of building. When the pieces arrived, they all fit together like a glove. When you see this you realize there is something very beautiful about working from abstract rules. If everyone works by them, and if all the material tolerances are observed, then making the building is all about agreements, codes, notations, not about construction in the conventional sense. **Speaks:** You are also now designing towers in Rotterdam? **Dubbeldam:** We started to research this project in 1997. The proposal was to take away a grain silo and replace it with three towers. I proposed a feasibility study to see how to reuse the silos in conjunction with new towers. My proposal was to use the existing grain silo as work/live units with parking below and to push the towers to cantilever over the edge of the water. The grain silo also forms a buffer zone between the newly proposed towers and an adjacent industrial zone. The three thirty-story residential towers cantilever off a platform over the river. The immense concrete footing continues in a structural and infrastructural spine that supports the towers. The structure of the towers needed to be flexible because it was not clear what unit size or arrangement the market would require over such a long period. We designed five different variations that could potentially be adapted for office space as well. The former harbor area has just been rezoned to mixed-use and the city is now very interested in the project as a kind of urban attractor that could reenergize the entire area.

This interview was originally published in "Design Intelligence," *a+u* 11, 2003.

REVITALIZATION STATEMENT A Housing Initiative for those Impacted by the Events of 9-11 and for the Rebuilding of Lower Manhattan: "…If you think about what would be the most appropriate ways to build for the future for those left behind and to remember the sacrifice that those 2,800 people who died at the World Trade Center site on September 11th, what could be better to memorialize them then to have housing, and schools, and cultural institutions, and retail—it all goes together and makes it a vibrant place…. They gave their lives so that we can live, let's live there….You want a mixture of housing. You have to have housing for the wealthy because they pay lots of taxes and they have a right to find housing, if they have the money and want to live better, more power to them. But not everybody is lucky enough to afford housing at any level. We've long ago made the decision as a compassionate society we're going to find a place for everybody to live….So you want to have all sorts of people at all sorts of economic levels…and that's what's beautiful about New York."
—Mayor Michael Bloomberg, July 19, 2002

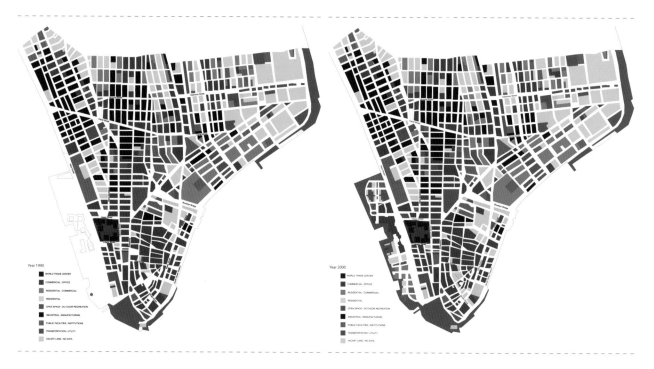

TYPOLOGIES New typologies are created: horizontal slabs for office spaces (not only more efficient but also psychologically more responsible); vertical structures for housing (allowing for privacy and expansive views). Flex Space provides amenities such as supermarkets, schools, and medical units, and Green Flex introduces parks, roof gardens, and playgrounds.

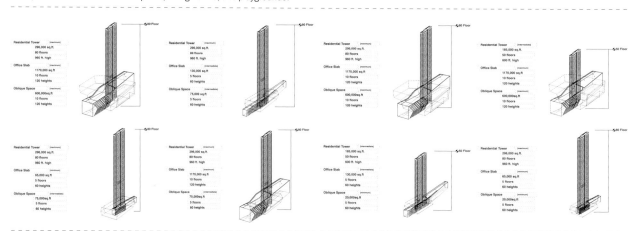

Flex-City

Type	Interactive installation
Location	Max Protetch Gallery, New York City; Biennale, Venice; Mob-Lab Biennale, Rotterdam
Year	2001, 2002, 2003

Shortly after the tragic events of September 11, 2001, we were invited to participate in the Max Protetch exhibition featuring proposals for a new World Trade Center. To us, the oversimplified super power strategy of "bigger and better," was extremely uninteresting, and a more humble, basic approach was necessary. It was an important time to rethink, rather than replace or rebuild, the twin towers—to rethink the shifting urban conditions and the future development of lower Manhattan. This would not only entail a different architecture, but also challenge what architecture stands for. We proposed an interactive think tank.

Within this global network, a new hybrid condition proliferates, in which the relationship between local and global is continually adjusting. Flex-City's interface allows one to create a cityscape sensitive to Social Flex and Econ Flex. It combines constant instability (stock market and migration patterns) with permanent adjustment (local politics and tourist behavior). Buildings are no longer envisioned as the physical manifestation of power, but as nodes in the global network of information systems, expressions of a democratic emancipated society. The new interactive model for downtown Manhattan is based on the idea that urban structures continually evolve with global economic and political forces. In today's market, consistency and stability have given way to uncertainty and volatility. For Flex-City, the evolution of the last ten years of economic flux was analyzed and interpreted as a consequence of growth, to be extrapolated into a future "flex" program.

In any given economic situation there are a number of possible outcomes or equilibria, any of which can establish and sustain itself. Consulting firms like Macroeconomic

Advisers use a computer model of the economy to produce forecasts of gross domestic product, inflation, unemployment, and other economic variables. Most variables are **EXOGENOUS**, meaning one has to assign values to them based on knowledge and intuition; for example, changed circumstances lead to changed behaviors. Successful forecasting involves three elements: science, art, and luck.

Flex-City is an interactive electronic environment in which development proposals are chosen, influenced, and ultimately created by the visitor/user. By selecting changes in certain logistic data (Econ Flex) and specific choice-driven data (Social Flex) the user generates one of the eighty-one scenarios for downtown Manhattan. This game environment not only introduces new **TYPOLOGIES**—horizontal slabs for commercial spaces, tall towers for apartments—but stresses Flex Space, which distributes schools, medical units, and supermarkets, and Green Flex, which creates parks, tree-lined streets, and playgrounds. New east/west infrastructures add the necessary "flex-ability."

The Flex-City interface reacts to the user's choices by "growing" the scenario on the screen, allowing one to observe it for a few seconds, then returning to the interface default. The idea was not to propose the perfect solution, but to allow one to understand the consequences of investment decisions and choice. The integrated Flex-Archive provides research data and background information on the changes in downtown over the last ten years in order to extrapolate the prognosis for the next ten years. The real flexibility will be found in the regeneration of a **HYBRID CITY MODEL** where mixed-use zones overlap and integrate in interlinked live/work/play/learn areas.

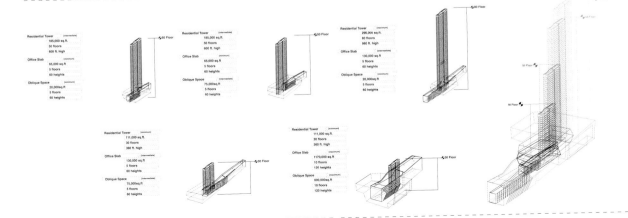

LOWER MANHATTAN POPULATION DATA 1990–2000 Populated
mostly by people who want to live close as possible to their jobs: 88%
are under 45, with 76% making over $90,000 a year, less than 10% have
children under 18//More than 56% of the city's population is foreign-born
or the children of foreign-born//Population increase between 1990–2000
of 9.4%//In 2010 projected a continuation of that rate: population of 8.8
million//Population density of 57 people per ha.
—New York City Department of City Planning

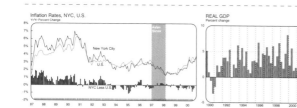
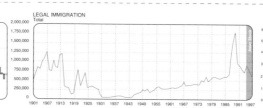

EXOGENOUS Any prognosis is exogenous, meaning dependent on knowledge (data) and intuition (choice). Here, research of a ten-year span (1990–2000) of lower Manhattan provides the data to extrapolate and project developments for the next ten years (2000–2010), in order to generate a Flex-City.

NEW YORK CITY RESOURCES DATA Commercial: Zoning and economic development decisions must focus on mixed-use solutions// Residential: Increase the number of housing units by at least 100,000; encourage new residential uses in manufacturing districts//Parks: Our waterfront is a major asset; a community garden policy must be established// Entertainment: Generates $25 billion in revenue//Tourism is critical to the city. —Mayor Michael Bloomberg, Election Campaign Statement, 2001

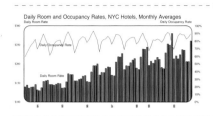

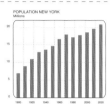

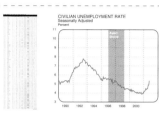

FLEX CITY CALCULATION MATRIX

01	1111	RECESSION	1	−	−	N/A	ENTERTAINMENT	C4 / R2	c −	R −	G −	PA −	I −	E +
02	2111	COMMUTING	2	±	−	PUBLIC	ENTERTAINMENT	C5 / R2	c ±	R −	G −	PA +	I −	E +
03	3111	WORK AND PLAY	3	+	−	PUBLIC	ENTERTAINMENT	C6 / R3	c +	R −	G −	PA +	I −	E +
04	1211	RECESSION	4	−	±	N/A	ENTERTAINMENT	C3 / R3	c −	R ±	G −	PA −	I −	E +
05	2211	MODERATE	5	±	±	PUBLIC	ENTERTAINMENT	C4 / R3	c ±	R ±	G −	PA +	I −	E +
06	3211	LIGHT CONGESTION	6	+	±	PUBLIC	ENTERTAINMENT	C5 / R4	c +	R ±	G −	PA +	I −	E +
07	1311	HIGHLY RESIDENTIAL	7	−	+	N/A	ENTERTAINMENT	C4 / R4	c −	R +	G −	PA −	I −	E +
08	2311	SOCIAL-FLEX	8	±	+	PUBLIC	ENTERTAINMENT	C5 / R4	c ±	R +	G −	PA +	I −	E +
09	3311	PLAY HARD	9	+	+	PUBLIC	ENTERTAINMENT	C6 / R5	c +	R +	G −	PA +	I −	E +
10	1211	RECESSION	1	−	−	N/A	ENTERTAINMENT	C3 / R2	c −	R −	G −	PA −	I −	E +
11	2121	COMMUTING	2	±	−	GREEN	ENTERTAINMENT	C4 / R2	c ±	R −	G +	PA −	I −	E +
12	3121	BALANCED WORK/PLAY	10	+	−	GREEN	ENTERTAINMENT	C5 / R3	c +	R −	G +	PA −	I −	E +
13	1221	RECESSION	4	−	±	N/A	ENTERTAINMENT	C2 / R3	c −	R ±	G −	PA −	I −	E +
14	2221	MODERATE	5	±	±	GREEN	ENTERTAINMENT	C3 / R3	c ±	R ±	G +	PA −	I −	E +
15	3221	MEDIUM HYBRID	11	+	±	GREEN	ENTERTAINMENT	C4 / R4	c +	R ±	G +	PA −	I −	E +
16	1321	HIGHLY RESIDENTIAL	7	−	+	N/A	ENTERTAINMENT	C3 / R4	c −	R +	G −	PA −	I −	E +
17	2321	PLAY	12	±	+	GREEN	ENTERTAINMENT	C4 / R4	c ±	R +	G +	PA −	I −	E +
18	3321	ECO-HYBRID	13	+	+	GREEN	ENTERTAINMENT	C5 / R5	c +	R +	G +	PA −	I −	E +
19	1131	RECESSION	1	−	−	N/A	ENTERTAINMENT	C3 / R3	c −	R −	G −	PA −	I −	E +
20	2131	COMMUTING	2	±	−	RESIDENTIAL	ENTERTAINMENT	C4 / R3	c ±	R −	G −	PA +	I −	E +
21	3131	OPTIMISTIC	14	+	−	RESIDENTIAL	ENTERTAINMENT	C5 / R4	c +	R −	G −	PA +	I −	E +
22	1231	RECESSION	4	−	±	N/A	ENTERTAINMENT	C2 / R4	c −	R ±	G −	PA −	I −	E +
23	2231	MODERATE	5	±	±	RESIDENTIAL	ENTERTAINMENT	C3 / R4	c ±	R ±	G −	PA +	I −	E +
24	3231	ECON-FLEX	15	+	±	RESIDENTIAL	ENTERTAINMENT	C4 / R5	c +	R ±	G −	PA +	I −	E +

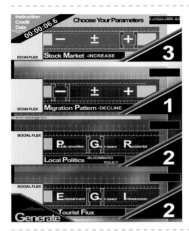

An interactive digital interface allows the visitor to create any of the 81 scenarios for Lower Manhattan by choosing parameters based on Social Flex (choice) and Econ Flex (data).

Ecological Explosion scenario: interface calculation (left) and result (below)

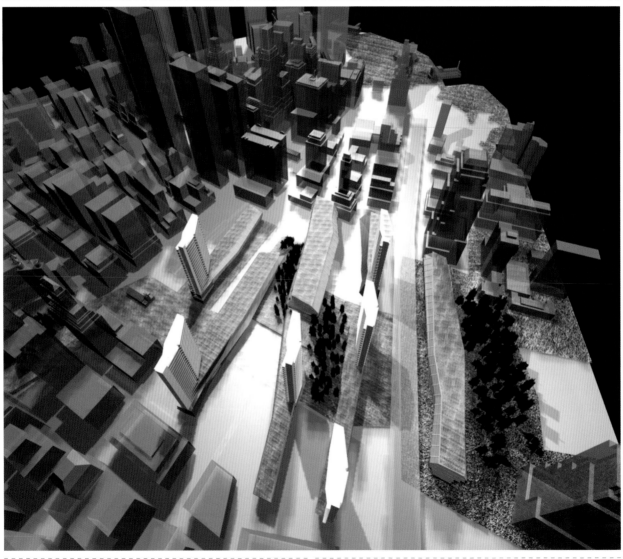

Baby Boom scenario: interface calculation (left) and result (below)

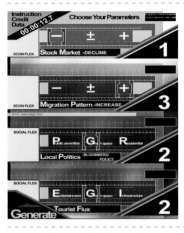

HYBRID CITY MODEL Replacing the monument, this area creates a hybrid city model for the New Yorker, integrating live, work, play, and learn zones.

Urban Jungle scenario:
interface calculation (left)
and result (below)

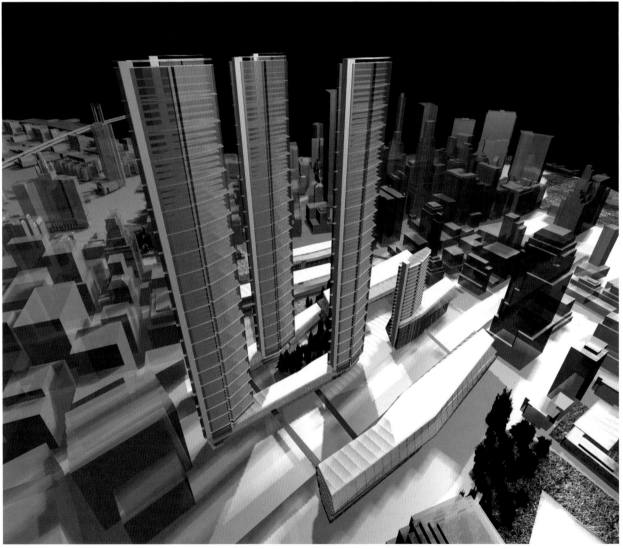

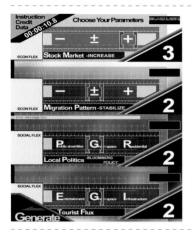

Housing in the Park scenario:
interface calculation (left)
and result (below)

Type   Urban redevelopment
           plan
Location   Schoonhoven,
           The Netherlands
Area   8.1 acres
Year   2003

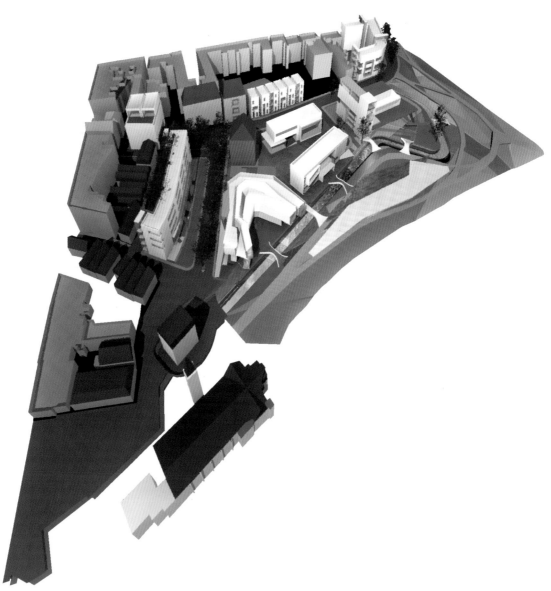

URBAN COUNTRYSIDE Schoonhoven is a medieval city (founded in 1322) located at the edge of the Green Heart—a government-protected green area in the middle of Holland that limits the outward growth of the cities that flank it, a measure to safeguard nature from the ever-spreading urban centers.

Schoonhoven Urban Design

The decision by the Dutch government to protect the Green Heart, the center of Holland, with the most green for an otherwise **URBAN COUNTRYSIDE** has challenging consequences for the cities that flank it. This extends to the city of Schoonhoven, which originated in the Middle Ages, obtaining its urban rights in 1322. Now the city council, faced with outward growth limitations, has begun to rethink part of the city center, an area known as Doelen Square.

The structure of Schoonhoven is actually a system of canals and lanes, not one of squares. A large tree-lined street originally ran through this site. This was later enlarged to a square and is now a cast-off back area primarily used for parking. This proposal returns to the city's founding structure, thus intensifying the density and usage of the Doelen Square area and reconnecting it to the rest of the center. The strategy redefines the urban infrastructure by widening the main streets, converting the parking lot back into a tree-lined lane with shops and restaurants, and integrating the existing park into the city and culture.

One important move is to give this part of the city its own destination, drawing in the large group of tourists already attracted to Schoonhoven. A proposed Silver and Glass Museum, indicative of the city's manufacturing history, is situated on the edge of the park, transforming this forgotten area into a "**MUSEUM PARK**," a cultural hub. The museum creates a link between the park, new shopping district, and city center. Its shop in the park, restaurant at the green lane, and cultural function will activate the area, becoming an integral whole. By collecting all the institutions, including the existing schools, at the edge, the park is further used by the citizens of Schoonhoven and forms a larger part of the system of green lanes already connected to it—a **GREEN NETWORK**. The publicly accessed courtyards of the institutions also link to the park, creating a mesmerizing path through the area.

A new housing unit is proposed that connects the low-density medieval streets to the more urban avenue of the museum park area. This "filter" building provides ateliers for artists at the remote back street side and modern living and shops at the museum park side. Additionally, new flexible single-family housing runs adjacent to the green avenue along the park. Spacious apartments gain direct access to the green zone and the shopping area around the museum. Constructed from a palette of natural materials, such as hardwood, zinc, and glass, these new housing units integrate with the great structures of earlier centuries, translated in a modern architecture.

 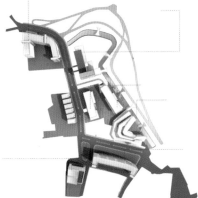 

Schoonhoven was always part of the Dutch network of trade routes; as it is located along the river, it had good connections and a lively culture in the form of its silver industry.

NETWORK CITY By restoring the area to a system of canals and tree-lined lanes and introducing a new museum/institutional district at the edge of the park, a green network of paths, courtyards, and park brings new life to Doelen Square.

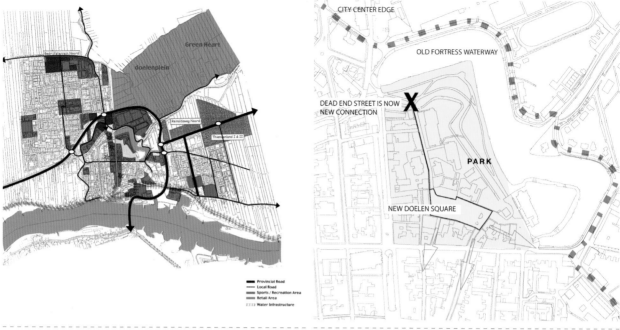

ATTRACTORS New programs activate the relationship between the park and the city center. Here, a housing complex for the elderly and two new schools attract diverse inhabitants and activities.

MUSEUM PARK The museum park establishes a new cultural hub that regenerates the city fabric into a comprehensive whole—the adaptation of the part influences the city as a whole.

Type	Mixed-use/residential towers
Location	Rotterdam, The Netherlands
Area	348,750 sq. ft.
Year	2000

1 NEW 30-STORY RESIDENTIAL TOWERS WITH SPLIT-LEVEL UNITS

2 NEW LIVING UNITS

3 COURTYARD WITH FITNESS CENTER AND PARKING BELOW

4 EXISTING SILO CONVERTED TO WORKSPACES

CONVERSION/INSERTION European cities centers are being redeveloped; industries move out, DINK's (double-income-no-kids) move in. Rotterdam's harbors are moving to the technologically advanced Europort, and the old harbor piers are now open for modern intervention. The Maas Harbor Pier is one of the last piers to be re-zoned. Live/work units will transform the existing landmark grain silo into an attractor for this dilapidated neighborhood, and three new towers will create magnificent apartments cantilevered over the Maas River.

Maashaven Towers

Working with a local developer and engineer, an urban redevelopment scheme is proposed for a harbor area south of Rotterdam's city center edge. Most harbor functions are relocating away from the city's core area to periphery industrial areas. The abandoned waterfront provides prime sites on the Maas River, such as Maashaven. Just one of the many piers that jut out in the river, the Maas Harbor Pier still contains several industrial structures, including a landmark grain silo—a remarkable example of 1930s Dutch concrete harbor construction by renowned architectural firm Brinkman & Van der Vlught. The proposal restores this structure and converts it to live/work units in combination with three new thirty-story (360-foot-high) residential towers that cantilever over the river. The economic and cultural impact of the development is planned to revitalize this now derelict part of Rotterdam.

CONVERSION: The monumental north wall of the silo is preserved and renovated, and the grain storage containers along the south side are removed, leaving an L-shaped structure of wall and plinth. A base of four stories for parking connects to the wall unit, which contains new office spaces. The base also carries apartments and an interior courtyard. The apartments are constructed in an open slab system of four- to six-story blocks and fabricated as a modular steel-and-glass panel wall structure—detailed with the precision of industrially designed filing cabinets—to integrate windows, doors, and interior balconies. The green courtyard contains sports facilities including tennis courts and a running track. The insertion of three glass stair and elevator towers and a maze of walkways and ramps transforms this industrial complex from a structure of interiority into a **NETWORK** of connectivity, also connecting to the three towers at the water's edge.

INSERTION: The new residential towers cantilever from the pier, negotiating the river and the city. Beginning with a generic tower, square in plan and what one would call a "**DEVELOPER'S DREAM**," the design of the buildings evolves in response to the specific site and positioning. A transformative process is used to adapt the shape of the structures; the towers stretch to allow for views and light on the grain silo, bend toward the river and city center, and inflate with program. The resulting form has crystalline qualities—a multifaceted glazed facade that reflects and refracts its surroundings and facilitates multiple views for the split-level apartments inside. The sculptural concrete base extends over the river and continues up as the core of the tower, asymmetrically placed toward the coastline, carrying the "light" volume of apartments.

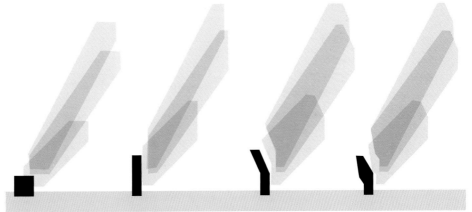

A square tower is the developer's dream. Not here. The three towers are transformed by the inflection of site forces. Their crystalline solids contain an internal atomic pattern specific for their siting; they are stretched over the waterline, bent toward the river and city center, and inflated with program.

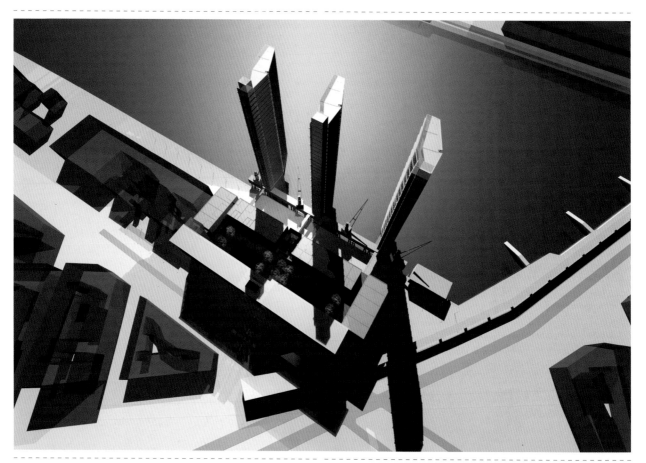

Double-height apartments are cantilevered over the river, suspended to view the city center from afar, at once removed and extremely well connected.

NETWORK The harbor's network system has been maintained; the renovated silo building is connected to the towers through a maze of paths, bridges, stairs, and elevators. This transforms the industrial complex from a structure of interiority into a network of connectivity. The silo is an open system in itself; freestanding housing units create an open inner elevated sports park with views of the river.

The section-cut reveals the
converted silo space; the
first four floors contain
generous parking spaces, a
raised park provides sporting
facilities, and interior
walkways connect all.

HIGH LINE FACTS Constructed 1929–34 // Spans 22 blocks, from 34th Street to Gansevoort Street // 1.45 miles long // 6.7 acres of space atop elevated rail deck // 30–60 feet wide and 18–30 feet high // Built to support two fully loaded freight trains // Primary construction materials: steel and reinforced concrete // Owners: Conrail/CSX Corporation
—compiled by Friends of the High Line

Adjustable light poles/extenders create lightscapes (above). Vertical parks generate access to the High Line with a multi-nodal art district, viewing tower, and market units (below).

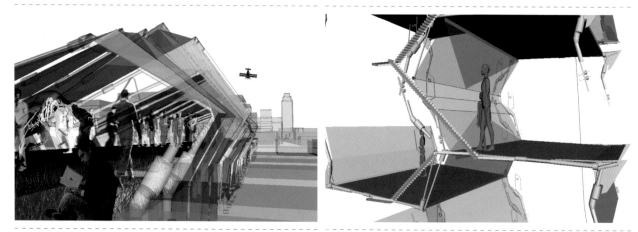

High Line

Type	Urban redevelopment; competition
Location	New York City
Area	6.7 acres
Year	2003

The High Line—a rusty, elevated railway constructed in the 1930s that hovers over Hell's Kitchen, West Chelsea, and the Meatpacking District in New York City—was a candidate for demolition as recently as 2000. Through the efforts of the preservationist group Friends of the High Line, the thirty-five-foot-high landmark structure will see new life as a 1.5-mile-long public park.

Considering its amazing location along the west side of Manhattan, flanking the Hudson River, and its scale, spanning twenty-two blocks, the remaining High Line segments could, and should, operate as an attractor for a new urban landscape. In a composite organizational strategy, rather than over-designing the massive rough steel structure, three main localities are designated as attractor points: the Meatpacking area, the Chelsea art district, and the final point at Penn Station. The High Line acts as a green zone that winds through the city on the elevated line. Vertical gardens as access points are created through stair and elevator entries and introduce the suspended park.

SPEED MARKET, MEATPACKING DISTRICT Here, the High Line is clamped by modular, adaptable units, or "clip-ons." A series of variables is used to create a Speed Market with multiple unit types. Each variation is designed to be flexible, operating on a cyclical basis to provide and explore new market opportunities—vegetables are located next to clothing, Internet booths, seating units, or even ATM machines, exploring the speed of urban life and digital networks. Where the High Line intersects with existing buildings, the units can be stored inside these structures during the ominous winter months. As the market demands, the nodes will expand along the edge of the Line. The canopies of each unit generate a floating topological landscape—a seasonal flag, which flowers when the temperature rises, advertising the start of spring (and the outdoor market). It is a place to shop and to interact with the site and the people that occupy it.

MULTINODAL ART DISTRICT, CHELSEA In this neighborhood, the High Line acts as generator emerging as a multinodal art point. A series of nomadic tent structures elevate the art world up over the district and provide an informed and informal overview. Special events animate the area, making exhibited artworks accessible to a larger and wider audience. Screens, projections, and interactive technology create an exciting virtual landscape, reflecting contemporary culture. A set of mechanically moving light poles, or extenders, connects all areas and forms an intriguing nightscape with ever-changing light patterns.

VIEWING TOWER, PENN STATION At Penn Station, the High Line bends up vertically into the sky and transforms into a tower, marking the end of the trail. Containing offices and viewing platforms, the tower represents a stoppage point and a normative deviation from the linear, horizontal movement. The creation of a totally open office space and flexible work environment allows the viewer to look back over the High Line, which is further abstracted in the tower's organic, adaptable steel structure. The tower is an observatory, a vertical hallway, and a new landmark.

This new mode for the High Line is based on the constant evolution of urban structures through global economic and political forces. The economic flux is interpreted as a consequence of growth to be extrapolated into a future "flex" program for the site—a flexible urban speed market for the New Yorker.

At the Meatpacking district clip-on market modules attach to the High Line structure—revisiting the market in an economical, political, and cultural sense. Market booth variations (below): tanning, vegetable, ATM, and viewing

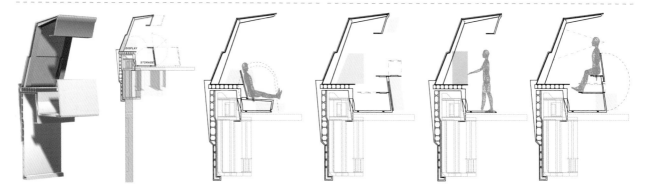

A site collage reveals the complexity of the High Line's relationship with adjacent buildings.

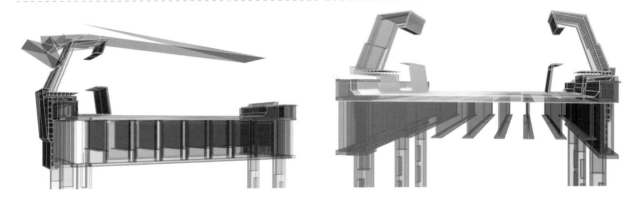

PANAMA DATA Population: 3,000,463//Area: slightly smaller than South Carolina; water: 853 sq mi. (2,210 sq km); land: 29,340 sq mi. (75,990 sq km); area total: 30,193 sq mi. (78,200 sq km)//Climate: tropical climate (up to 86% humidity and 79 °F [26 °C] annual average), with periods of rain and sunshine alternating throughout the year//Bocas del Toro: latitude: 9,416667; 9° 25' 0 N; longitude: -82,51667; 82° 31' 0 W; 175 mi. (280 km) west of Panama City

Type	Resort/residences
Location	Shepherds Island; Bocas del Toro, Panama
Area	2,500 sq. ft.
Year	2004–05

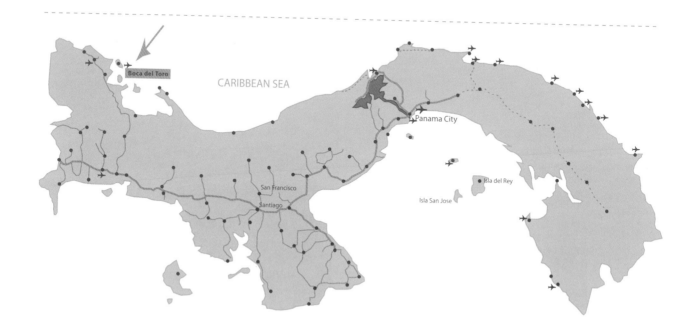

SELF-SUFFICIENT The new eco resort is self-sufficient; its tourist and service community are based on eco systems and independent infrastructures. Ten villas are built on piers in the small bay, a restaurant and bar hover over the water, and spa and meditation facilities are located on the wooded hills of the island.

Eco Resort Panama

The inherent memory of an island as an organic unit constitutes a permanently unstable entity, an ever-fluctuating form, a constantly evolving structure. The archipelago of Bocas del Toro located on Panama's northwestern Caribbean coast is an exceptional site with spectacular coral reefs and warm, crystal-clear waters. Discovered by Christopher Columbus in 1502, the town of Bocas del Toro is the center of activity in the islands. Most of the people in the area are Afro-Caribbean; the rest of the population is made up of Guaymi Indian, European (recently arrived and also descendants from the early banana industry boom), and a handful of U.S. expatriates. It is an unassuming, sleepy, relaxed town. The client, originally from New York, has fallen in love with the area and has acquired one-third of Shepherds Island to construct a **SELF-SUFFICIENT** eco resort. The island, across the bay from Bocas, consists of a very steep hillside with amazing tropical fruit trees and a small bay on a gorgeous coral reef; there is no beach (yet).

The introduction of several pier structures on the waterside of the property will cause a gradual settlement of sand particles along that boundary and the growth of a naturally protected beach. The piers also provide the foundations for cabin-type buildings—temporal dwellings, balancing on the edge of the stable and unstable region. The minimal cabins feature large terraces and undulating roofs that produce shade, shield from the tropical rain, and create privacy. Forming horizontal bands of private space, the structures are suspended over and from the piers, their hovering floor planes reflected in the flat, supple surface of the water. An adjacent restaurant/bar area intertwines and mediates the boundary between the private and public space.

The higher sector of the island property will contain services such as sports facilities, shops, a spa, and yoga meditation spaces. The structures on this landside confront an extremely steep geographical condition. Rather than fight this severe site, the buildings follow the landscape, their floor plates bending with and forming to the undulating ground. In contrast, the roof planes create a level datum, a reference to the surface of the surrounding water.

The ocean as a striated system is measured, mapped, and navigated creating the basis for the diverse resort buildings. These two **INVERSE TYPOLOGIES**, the low-lying private cabins and the elevated public commercial/recreation structures, play off of each other, reflecting the differing building conditions and challenging topological strata. New horizons supplement the existing landscape in an integral subversive way.

The assemblage of the structures follows the traditional construction methods of the area, with natural ventilation systems, overhanging roofs, water collection and distribution, and farming. The local woods and surrounding bamboo are water treated, easy to bend, and capable of dealing with the heavy tropical climate. Foundations are poured in concrete to ensure that the more delicate wood surfaces do not touch the ground or water and will survive the intense conditions. Drawings, devised as assembly manuals, explain the basics of the component part construction method for the local craftsmen and builders. The information is image based and easy to understand—a memory system more than a construction document; interpretation is encouraged and, partially, expected.

INVERSE TYPOLOGIES The land-based structures and the cabins located over the water have inverted typologies. On land, the buildings initiate a new datum; flat roofs juxtapose undulating floor surfaces, following the slope of the hill. The opposite occurs at the ocean side, the water-based cabins feature undulating roofs—smooth surfaces that protect from the rain and sunshine—and even floor planes.

The owner's house is located on the steep hill overlooking the bay. Its supple split-level structure features a large cantilevering roof and creates a modern environment with a local material expression.

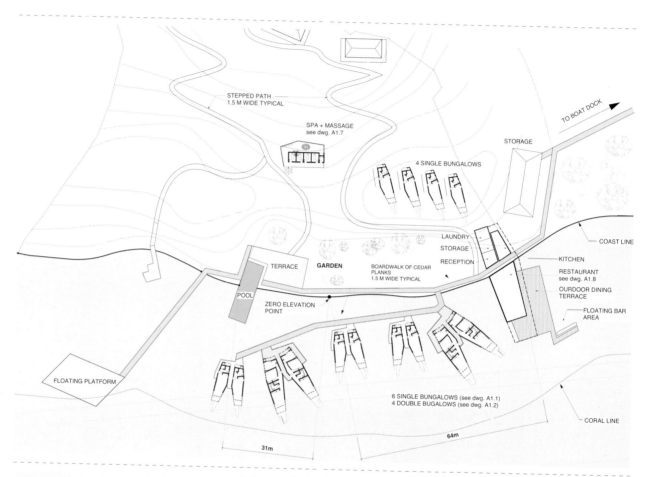

STEPPED PATH
1.5 M WIDE TYPICAL

SPA + MASSAGE
see dwg. A1.7

TO BOAT DOCK

STORAGE

4 SINGLE BUNGALOWS

COAST LINE

TERRACE GARDEN

LAUNDRY
STORAGE
RECEPTION

KITCHEN

BOARDWALK OF CEDAR
PLANKS
1.5 M WIDE TYPICAL

RESTAURANT
see dwg. A1.8

POOL

OURDOOR DINING
TERRACE

ZERO ELEVATION
POINT

FLOATING BAR
AREA

FLOATING PLATFORM

6 SINGLE BUNGALOWS (see dwg. A1.1)
4 DOUBLE BUGALOWS (see dwg. A1.2)

CORAL LINE

31m

64m

Panama House

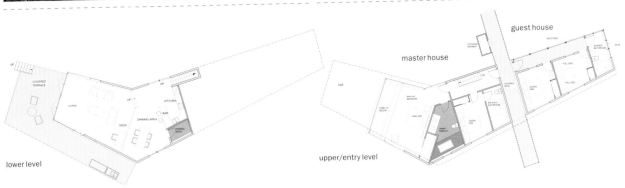

lower level

upper/entry level

master house

guest house

Local materials such as hard-
woods and bamboo, inventive
attachment methods, and simple
decorations have been rein-
troduced in a low maintenance
exterior shell that filters
light and provides great views.

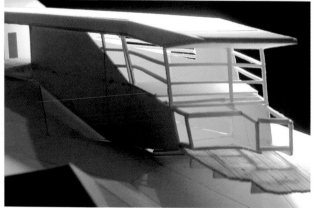

The skin of the residences is made of wood slats that allow air to filter through. The flat roofs slope to catch rainwater—the only supply of fresh water apart from the island's small spring.

AT Acknowledgments

I would like to thank the whole Archi-Tectonics team throughout the years, the clients, contractors, and engineers who have donated their love, inspiration, and patience to the hard process of architecture. Great thanks go to the team who worked on the AT Index: the writers, Michael Speaks, Javier Barreiro Cavestany, Detlef Mertins, and Reed Kroloff, who wrote straight through Hurricane Katrina while in exile in Houston; the great designers Cornelia Blatter and Marcel Hermans of Coma; the Princeton Architectural Press staff, with special thanks to Megan Carey, who moved cities, apartments, and jobs and kept working on it throughout; and, of course, Jonathan Jackson, my partner in the production of the book, who helped select, construct, and collect the images that ultimately became this Index. The biggest support team is a small but strong one, my parents, Mieke and Cor who have been incredible throughout the different schools, jobs, and travels, with their wise, calm, loving advice and support. Last but not least, a big thank you to my great group of friends, who are my family and home away from home. Thank you all for now and ever!

AT Contributors

Javier Barreiro Cavestany is the author of poems and stories, texts for stage and screen, and articles and essays. He has published three books of poetry: *Animal sin manada* (Mexico City, 2000), *Voces para una batalla* (Mexico City, 1994), and *Tecnicas de sobrevivencia* (Buenos Aires, 1987). He is director of the publishing project *Ex Libris* and is a staff editor of the architecture magazine *Arquine*. He lives in Mexico City.

COMA, founded by Cornelia Blatter and Marcel Hermans, is a design studio based in Amsterdam and Brooklyn, NY. They conceptualize, art direct, design, and produce work in various media ranging from print to the Internet to environments. Some of COMA's recent projects include the art direction and design of *Frame* magazine; *Hella Jongerius* for Phaidon Press; *Bruce Nauman: Theaters of Experience* for the Guggenheim Museum; *Rhythm Science* by Paul D. Miller (aka DJ Spooky that Subliminal Kid) for The MIT Press; *Architectural Laboratories: Greg Lynn & Hani Rashid* for NAi; and a multimedia presentation of architectural models by John M. Johansen for Stroom, the Hague's visual arts center. In addition to maintaining their design practice, they are enthusiastic educators who lecture at professional conferences and teach at institutions including Yale School of Art, Art Center College of Design, and Merz Academy in Stuttgart.

Reed Kroloff is the Dean of the Tulane University School of Architecture and an independent architectural consultant and commentator. The recipient of the American Academy in Rome's 2003 Rome Prize Fellowship, Kroloff previously served as Editor-in-Chief of *Architecture* magazine. Prior to joining *Architecture* in 1995, he taught at Arizona State University, where he was a tenured professor, and the Assistant Dean. At ASU, he received the first-ever "Award for Academic Excellence" from the Arizona chapter of the AIA. Kroloff advises a range of clients on architect selection and design strategy, including, among others, the U.S. Army Corps of Engineers, the Ministry of Culture of the Federal Government of Mexico, the Whitney Museum of American Art, the University of Connecticut, and Motown Center. He writes and lectures widely, and is a regular visiting critic at architecture schools and professional organizations across the country. He holds degrees from the University of Texas at Austin and Yale University, and has practiced architecture in Texas and Arizona. Kroloff serves on numerous boards and advisory councils, ranging from the Register of Peer Professionals of the United States General Services Administration to the Public Architecture Foundation.

Detlef Mertins is Professor and Chair of the Architecture Department at the University of Pennsylvania. He is an architect, historian, and critic whose revisionist interpretations of modernism have been widely published in journals, anthologies, and exhibition catalogs. He is editor of *The Presence of Mies* and the English edition of Walter Curt Behrendt's *The Victory of the New Building Style*. Recent publications include contributions to Charles Waldheim's *CASE: Lafayette Park*, Lars Spuybroek's *NOX* and Foreign Office Architects' *Phylogenesis: FOA's Arc*.

Michael Speaks is a Los Angeles–based educator, researcher, and writer. He has published and lectured internationally on contemporary art, architecture, urban design, and scenario planning. Former Director of the Graduate Program and the Metropolitan Research and Design Post Graduate Program at the Southern California Institute of Architecture in Los Angeles, Speaks has also taught in the graphic design department at the Yale School of Art and in the architecture programs at Harvard University, Columbia University, The University of Michigan, Parsons School of Design, The Berlage Institute, and the TU Delft. Speaks is founding editor of the cultural journal *Polygraph* and former editor at *Any* in New York, and he is currently a contributing editor for *Architectural Record* as well as an editorial advisory board member of *a+u*.

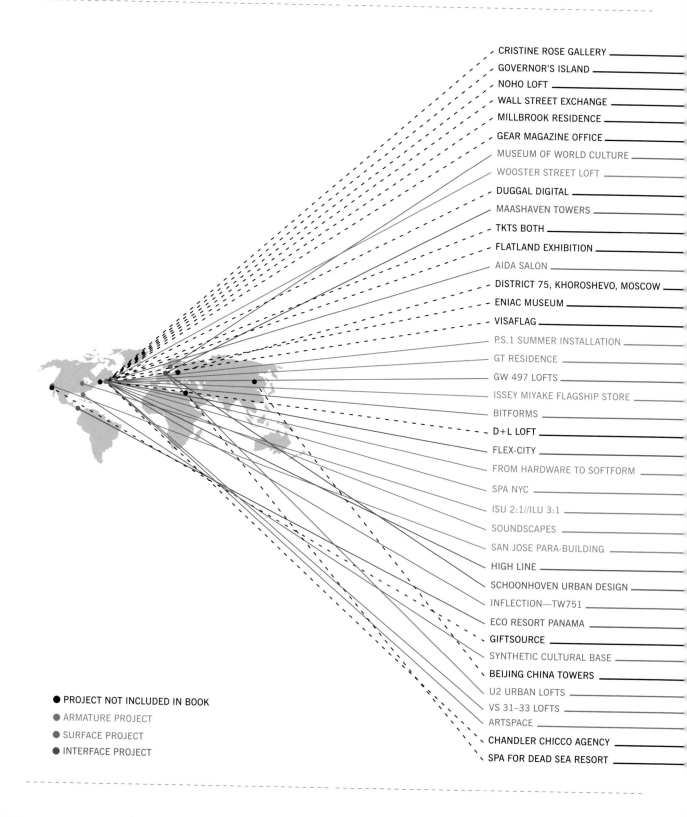

CRISTINE ROSE GALLERY
GOVERNOR'S ISLAND
NOHO LOFT
WALL STREET EXCHANGE
MILLBROOK RESIDENCE
GEAR MAGAZINE OFFICE
MUSEUM OF WORLD CULTURE
WOOSTER STREET LOFT
DUGGAL DIGITAL
MAASHAVEN TOWERS
TKTS BOTH
FLATLAND EXHIBITION
AIDA SALON
DISTRICT 75, KHOROSHEVO, MOSCOW
ENIAC MUSEUM
VISAFLAG
P.S.1 SUMMER INSTALLATION
GT RESIDENCE
GW 497 LOFTS
ISSEY MIYAKE FLAGSHIP STORE
BITFORMS
D+L LOFT
FLEX-CITY
FROM HARDWARE TO SOFTFORM
SPA NYC
ISU 2:1//ILU 3:1
SOUNDSCAPES
SAN JOSE PARA-BUILDING
HIGH LINE
SCHOONHOVEN URBAN DESIGN
INFLECTION—TW751
ECO RESORT PANAMA
GIFTSOURCE
SYNTHETIC CULTURAL BASE
BEIJING CHINA TOWERS
U2 URBAN LOFTS
VS 31–33 LOFTS
ARTSPACE
CHANDLER CHICCO AGENCY
SPA FOR DEAD SEA RESORT

● PROJECT NOT INCLUDED IN BOOK
● ARMATURE PROJECT
● SURFACE PROJECT
● INTERFACE PROJECT

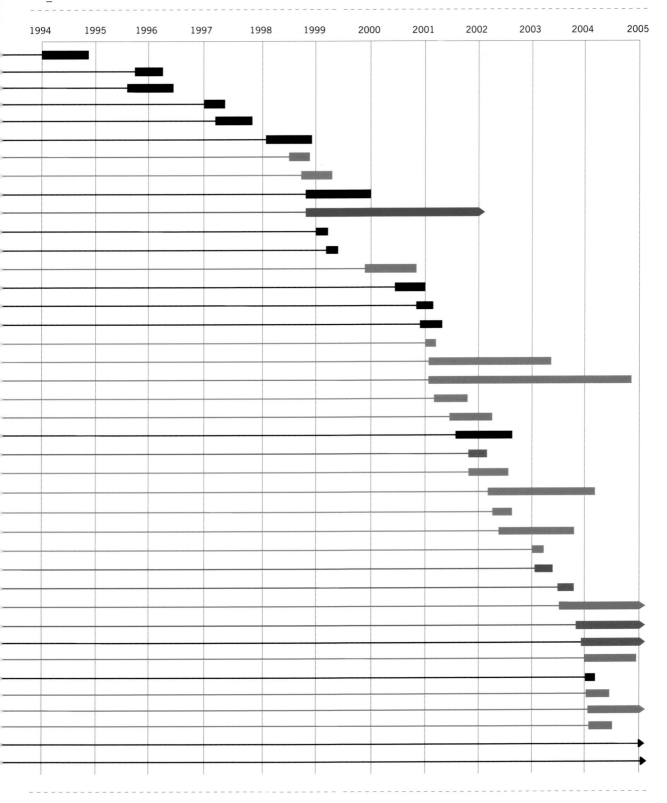

AT Credits

Armature

GT Residence, 2002

Client: Michael H. Spain
Principal in charge: Winka Dubbeldam
Project leader: Michael
Hundsnurscher
Team: Tanja Bitzer, Aaron Brakke,
Rob Henderson, Philip Holley, Sung
Kyun Im, Michael Johnston, Kajsa
Krause, Sebastian Saint Jean
Consultants: Contractor: T & L
Construction; Contractors for zinc
roofing, fenestration, and railings:
UAD Group; Structural engineer:
Buro Happold; Mechanical engineer:
Stanislav Slutsky, PE
Photography: Floto + Warner
Photography and Archi-Tectonics

Guest House Carmel, 2001

Client: Michael H. Spain
Principal in charge: Winka Dubbeldam
Project leader: Michael
Hundsnurscher
Team: Rob Henderson, Sung Kyun
Im, Kajsa Krause
Consultants: Contractor: T & L
Construction; Structural engineer:
Buro Happold; Mechanical engineer:
Stanislav Slutsky, PE
Photography: Floto + Warner
Photography and Archi-Tectonics

From *Hard*Ware to Soft*Form*, 2002

In collaboration with: Ted Selker,
Winslow Burleson, and Ernesto
Arroyo of the Context Awareness
Group of the MIT Media Lab,
Cambridge
Principal in charge: Winka Dubbeldam
Team: Susanne Bellinghausen,
Michael Hundsnurscher, Ana Sotrel,
Leo Yung, Ana Zatezalo
Consultants: Digital programming:
Als Design, Seiichi Saito; Interactive
components: Beatrize Witzgall;
Sound design: Jesus Colao Martinez
Sponsors: The Netherlands
Foundation for Visual Arts, Design
and Architecture; Steelcase Inc.
NYC; The Dutch Consulate of New
York
Photography: Elliott Kaufman and
Archi-Tectonics

Spa NYC, 2004

Client: Spa Development Partners.
Principal in charge: Winka Dubbeldam
Team: Brooks Atwood, Ana Sotrel,
Ana Zatezalo

ISU 2:1//ILU 3:1, 2002

Client: Walker Art Center
Principal in charge: Winka Dubbeldam
Team: Rob Henderson, Michael
Hundsnurscher, Sung Kyun Im

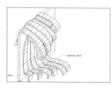

P.S.1 Summer Installation, 2001

Client: P.S.1
Principal in charge: Winka Dubbeldam
Team: Tanja Bitzer, Aaron Brakke,
Michael Hundsnurscher, Sebastian
Saint Jean

**SoundScapes, October 2003–April
2004**

In collaboration with: Robert Mion Jr.,
IMI Master Craftworker
Client: National Building Museum
Curator: Stanley Tigerman
Principal in charge: Winka Dubbeldam
Project leader: Ana Zatezalo
Team: Michael Hundsnurscher, Serra
Kiziltan, Adam Marcus, Jesus Colao
Martinez, Chas Peppers
Consultants: Sound Design: Jesus
Colao Martinez
Photography: Archi-Tectonics

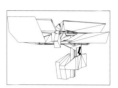

San Jose Para-building, 2003

Client: San Jose State University
Principal in charge: Winka Dubbeldam
Team: Michael Hundsnurscher, Ana
Sotrel, Ana Zatezalo

Issey Miyake Flagship Store, 2000

Client: Miyake America
Principal in charge: Winka Dubbeldam
Team: Michael Hundsnurscher, Serra
Kiziltan, Ana Zatezalo

Wooster Street Loft, 1998

Client: Jonathon Carroll
Principal in charge: Winka Dubbeldam
Team: Marcus Acheson, Joachim
Karelse, Bernard Kornberger,
Roemer Pierik, Stephen Roe
Consultants: Contractor: A.J.
Greenwich Contracting; Structural
engineer: Severud Associates;
Mechanical engineer: Stanislav
Slutsky, PE
Photography: Paul Warchol
Photography, Michael Moran,
Christopher Kicherer, and Mark
Seelen (with styling/production by
Mark Heldens)

Surface

GW 497 Lofts, 2004

Client: Take One LLC, Jonathon
Carroll
Principal in charge: Winka Dubbeldam
Architect of record: David Hotson,
Architect
Project leader: Ana Sotrel
Team: Nicola Bauman, Tanja Bitzer,
Amy Farina, Michael Hundsnurscher,
Deborah Kully, Stacey Mariash, Ty
Tikari, Beatrice Witzgall, Leo Yung
Consultants: General contractor:
York Hunter Construction Services;
Structural engineer: Buro Happold;
Mechanical engineer: Gabor
M. Szakal Engineers; Curtain
wall consultant: Israel Berger &
Associates, Bill Logan; Acoustic
consultant: Shen Milsom & Wilke;
Elevator consultant: Barker
Mohandas
Photography: Floto + Warner
Photography, Esto Photography, and
Archi-Tectonics

VS 31–33 Lofts, 2004

Client: Vestry Acquisitions LLC
Principal in charge: Winka Dubbeldam
Architect of record: Michael Zenreich
Architect
Team: Thomas Barry, Jordan Bartlett,
Lucie Flather, Wouter Van Daele,
Jose Munoz Villers
Consultants: Structural engineer:
WSP Cantor Seinuk; Mechanical
engineer: Stanislav Slutsky, PE;

Aida Salon, 2000

Client: Aida Alvarado
Principal in charge: Winka Dubbeldam
Team: Lissa Desbarattes, Ty Tikari
Consultants: Contractor: A.J.
Greenwich Contracting; Mechanical
engineer: Stanislav Slutsky, PE
Photography: Paul Warchol
Photography

Museum of World Culture, 1998

Client: Museum of World Culture
Principal in charge: Winka Dubbeldam
Team: Michael Hundsnurscher,
Stephen Roe, Sebastian Saint Jean

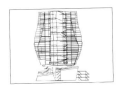

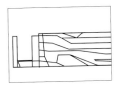

Synthetic Cultural Base, 2003

Client: private
Principal in charge: Winka Dubbeldam
Team: Dominique Meier, Masako
Saito, Ana Zatezalo

ArtSpace, 2004

Principal in charge: Winka Dubbeldam
Team: Brooks Atwood, Eun Suk Oh,
Alex Pincus, Ana Zatezalo

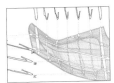

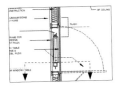

Inflection—TW751, 2005

Client: Ivalo Lighting Incorporated
Principal in charge: Winka Dubbeldam
Team: Jose Munoz Villers, Ana
Zatezalo
Photography: Ivalo and Archi-
Tectonics

U2 Urban Lofts, 2004

Principal in charge: Winka Dubbeldam
Local architect: Rokus Visser
Architects
Team: Ana Zatezalo

Bitforms, 2001

Client: Bitforms Gallery, Steven
Sacks
Principal in charge: Winka Dubbeldam
Team: Peter Jahnke, Seiichi Saito
Consultants: General contractor: A.J.
Greenwich Contracting; Aluminum
and Plexiglas walls: UAD Group
Photography: Addison Thompson and
Archi-Tectonics

Interface

Flex-City, 2001, 2002, 2003

Principal in charge: Winka Dubbeldam
Team: Sung Kyun Im, Seiichi Saito,
Leo Yung
Consultants: Investment consulting:
Jonathon Carroll; Sound design:
Emanuel Ruffler
Sponsors/Exhibition object: UAD
Group

Schoonhoven Urban Design, 2003

Client: City of Schoonhoven
Principal in charge: Winka Dubbeldam
Local architect: Rokus Visser
Architects
Team: Brooks Atwood, Serra Kiziltan,
Adam Marcus, Chas Peppers, Ana
Zatezalo

Maashaven Towers, 2000

Principal in charge: Winka Dubbeldam
Local architect: Rokus Visser
Architects
Team: Michael Hundsnurscher,
Roemer Pierik, Shirley Smit, Mikkel
Stubgaard, Ana Zatezalo

High Line, 2003

Client: Friends of the High Line
Principal in charge: Winka Dubbeldam
Team: Serra Kiziltan, Stacey
Mariash, Ana Zatezalo

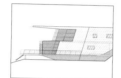

Eco Resort Panama/Panama House, 2005

Client: Lee Glaser
Principal in charge: Winka Dubbeldam
Team: Francoise Akinosho, Dwayne
Dancy, Tomasz Marchewka, Ana
Sotrel
Photography: Archi-Tectonics

Additional

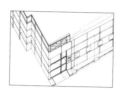

Cristine Rose Gallery, 1994

Type: Interactive installation; and
facade renovation
Location: New York City
Principal in charge: Winka Dubbeldam
Consultants: Contractor: JK Interior
Design; Structural engineer: Peter
J. Galdi

Governor's Island, 1996

Type: Competition, honorable
mention
Location: Governors Island, New
York City
Area: 212 acres
Client: Van Alen Institute
Principal in charge: Winka Dubbeldam
Team: Phillip Mohr, Ivo Nelissen, Julie
Schurtz

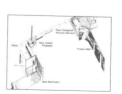

Noho Loft, 1996

Type: Residential loft
Location: New York City
Area: 2,500 sq. ft.
Principal in charge: Winka Dubbeldam
Team: Stephen Roe
Consultants: Contractor: J.N.
Construction; Structural engineer:
Peter J. Galdi
Photography: Eduard Hueber

Millbrook Residence, 1997

Type: Residence
Location: New York
Area: 3,500 sq. ft.
Principal in charge: Winka Dubbeldam
Team: Julie Schurtz
Consultants: Structural engineer:
Guy Nordenson and Associates
Exhibited in The Un-Private House at
MoMA in 1999

Gear Magazine Office, 1998

Type: Office
Location: New York City
Area: 8,000 sq. ft.
Principal in charge: Winka Dubbeldam
Team: Stephen Roe
Consultants: Contractor: Tectonix;
Mechanical engineer: Empiretech
Consulting
Photography: Marijke de Gruyter

Duggal Digital, 1999

Type: Digital imaging facility
Location: New York City
Area: 24,000 sq. ft.
Principal in charge: Winka Dubbeldam
Team: Kenny Endo, Michael
Hundsnurscher, Meghna Patel,
Roemer Pierik, Stephen Roe
Consultants: Structural engineer:
Severud Associates; Mechanical
engineer: IB Consulting Engineers
Photography: Michael Moran

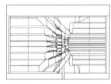

Flatland Exhibition, 1999

Type: Installation
Location: Frederieke Taylor Gallery,
New York City; TZ Art Gallery
Area: 168,000 sq. ft.
Principal in charge: Winka Dubbeldam
Team: Stephen Roe

TKTS Booth, 1999

Type: Ticket booth; competition
Location: Times Square, New York
City
Area: 700 sq. ft.
Client: Van Alen Institute
Principal in charge: Winka Dubbeldam
Team: Kenny Endo, Meghna Patel

Eniac Museum, 2001

Type: Museum
Location: Philadelphia
Area: 5,600 sq. ft.
Client: Engineering School, University
of Pennsylvania
Principal in charge: Winka Dubbeldam
Team: Michael Hundsnurscher

Visafslag, 2001

Type: Restaurant
Location: Scheveningen, Holland
Area: 3,800 sq. ft.
Client: private
Principal in charge: Winka Dubbeldam

D+L Loft, 2002

Type: Residential loft
Location: New York City
Area: 3,500 sq. ft.
Principal in charge: Winka Dubbeldam
Team: Ulrike Franzel, Sung Kyun Im,
Stacey Mariash
Consultants: Contractor: A.J.
Greenwich Contracting; Fiberglass
walls: Panelite; Kitchen: Valcucine
Photography: James Wilkens

Giftsource, 2005

Type: Hotel shop concept
Area: 1,500 sq. ft.
Client: Mr. Alvarado
Principal in charge: Winka Dubbeldam
Team: Ana Zatezalo

Schein Apartment, 2005

Type: Residential loft design
Location: New York City
Area: 3,000 sq. ft.
Client: Peter Schein
Principal in charge: Winka Dubbeldam
Project leader: Bittor Sanchez-
Monasterio
Team: Brooks Atwood, Ana Sotrel
Consultants: Mechanical engineer:
Stanislav Slutsky, PE

American Loft Building, 2006

Type: Residential building
Location: Philadelphia
Area: 63,000 sq. ft.
Client: Crei, LLC
Principal in charge: Winka Dubbeldam
Project leader: Bittor Sanchez-
Monasterio
Team: Pilar Echezarreta, Christina
Tung, Patrick Wong
Architect of record: Landmark
Professional Design Inc.
Consultants: Structural engineer:
Cantor Seinuk; Mechanical engineer:
BHG Consulting, Inc.

Spike Building, 2007

Type: Residential building
Location: New York City
Area: 70,000 sq. ft.
Client: Puissance Enterprises, LLC
Principal in charge: Winka Dubbeldam
Team: Bittor Sanchez-Monasterio,
Wouter Van Daele, Jose Munoz
Villers, Patrick Wong
Architect of record: Michael Zenreich
Architect
Consultants: Structural engineer:
Cantor Seinuk

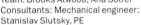

Published by Princeton Architectural Press
37 East Seventh Street, New York, New York 10003

For a free catalog of books, call 1.800.722.6657
Visit our web site at www.papress.com

Editor: Megan Carey
Concept and Design: COMA Amsterdam/New York, www.comalive.com
Project assistant: Jonathan Jackson

Publication of this book is supported in part by a grant from
The Netherlands Foundation for Visual Arts, Design and Architecture.

Image Credits: All imagery courtesy Archi-Tectonics unless otherwise noted.
Floto+Warner: 25l, 29bl, 29br, 30br, 31ml, 31mr, 32 all, 33b, 81, 82, 83,
84–85, 110b, 111bl, 111br, 112b, 113b, 114tl, 114tml, 114tmr, 114bl,
115tl, 115tm, 115tr, 161, 162, 163, 164, 165; Elliott Kaufman: 40b, 41b,
172–73, 174–75; Michael Moran: 88, 89; Mark Seelen (with styling/produc-
tion by Mark Heldens): 76tl, 76tr, 76bml, 76bmr, 76br, 77bl, 77br; Space
Imaging: 180 all, 190b; Addison Thompson: 92–93, 94–95, 96, 155b;
Albert Vecerka/Esto: 108tl, 108tr; Paul Warchol: 76bl, 77tl, 77tr, 78tl, 78tr,
79tl, 79tr, 86–87, 90, 91, 140t, 141br, 144, 145t, 166–67, 168, 169, 170–71

Library of Congress Cataloging-in-Publication Data

Dubbeldam, Winka.
 Archi-Tectonics index / Winka Dubbeldam ; introduction by Reed Kroloff ;
contributions by Javier Barreiro Cavestany ... [et al.].
   p. cm.
 ISBN 1-56898-535-5 (hardcover : alk. paper)
1. Dubbeldam, Winka—Catalogs. 2. Archi-Tectonics (Firm)—Catalogs. 3.
Architectural practice, International—Catalogs. 4. Architecture,
Modern—20th century—Catalogs. 5. Architecture, Modern—21st
century—Catalogs. 6. Architecture—Technological innovations—Catalogs.
I. Barreiro, Javier, 1959- II. Archi-Tectonics (Firm) III. Title.
   NA1153.D79A4 2005
   720.92—dc22
             2005021807

Marcus Acheson Franc
Nicola Bauman Susann
Lissa Desbarattes Win
Lucie Flather Monty Fo
Michael Hundsnurscher
Kagerbauer Joachim Ka
Kyu Philippe Lacher Ri
Martinez Shannon Mat
Meghna Patel Chas Pe
de Riquelme Stephen F
Sanchez-Monasterio Ju
Stubgaard Ty Tikari Ch
Weve Aaron White Be

coise Akinosho Brooks Atv

ne Bellinghausen Tanja Bit

ka Dubbeldam Pilar Eche

rman Ulrike Franzel Doria

r Sung Kyun Im Jonathan

arelse Serra Kiziltan Berr

ma Marcel Tomasz Marc

ther Dominique Meier Pl

ppers Tom Pierce Roeme

Roe Lovisa Rottier Sebas

ulie Schurtz Dongmin Shi

ristina Tung Wouter Van

eatrice Witzgall Patrick V

ood **Daniel Barber** Thoma
er **Aaron Brakke** Giorgio
arreta **Constanze Elges** K
Gray **Rob Henderson** Phili
ackson **Peter Jahnke** Mic
rd **Kornberger** Kajsa Kraus
ewka **Adam Marcus** Stace
lip **Mohr** Illich Mujica Iv
Pierik **Alex Pincus** Sebast
an **Saint Jean** Masako Sa
Jasmin **Shorter** Shirley S
aele **Jose Munoz Villers** M
ong **Leo Yung** Natalie Za

s Barry Jordan Bartlett
3runetti Dwayne Dancy
Kenny Endo Amy Farina
ip Holley Casey Hughes
hael Johnston Andreas
se Deborah Kully Dong
ey Mariash Jesus Colao
o Nelissen Eun Suk Oh
ian Queney Gregory M.
ito Seiichi Saito Bittor
mit Ana Sotrel Mikkel
Maarten Wessel Nicole
nnettou Ana Zatezalo